HEAD2HEAD

Paul Gilbert

Author Publishing Ltd
61 Gainsborough Road, Felixstowe,
Suffolk IP11 7HS

ISBN 1 898030 55 3

British Library Cataloguing in
Publication Data available.

Cover design by Cathi Stevenson

Produced in Milton Keynes
by Lightning Source

To

Lisa, Chloe and Olivia

with love

Contents

PAUL GILBERT

Paul Gilbert is the Chief Executive and Legal Director of LawBook Consulting ("LBC"), a specialist training and management consultancy company for law firms and in-house legal teams both in the UK and internationally. LBC specialises in relationship management issues, value-adding initiatives, strategic planning and staff development.

Previously Paul was Group Company Secretary at United Assurance Group PLC and head of legal services for Cheltenham & Gloucester plc. He has also held positions as chairman and chief executive of the Law Society Commerce & Industry Group. He has served as a director to the Legal Practice Course Board and as a non-executive Chairman of a pension trustee company. He is a Law Society Council Member and sits on the Law Society's main management board. He is also a trustee of the Solicitors Pro Bono Group.

Acknowledgements

I would like to thank all the people involved in helping to write this book, including all the solicitors and clients who gave their time so helpfully in interviews and for my research. I would particularly like to thank the following lawyers who were especially generous with their time.

Keith Ford
Ann Page
Tina Morgan
Michael Morris
Graham Howell
Nathalie Schwarz
Lawrence Smith
John Thurwell
John Ellison

All case studies, anecdotes etc have been anonymised and some facts changed to ensure confidentiality.

I would like to thank LawBook Consulting's administration manager, Dawn Jones, without whose patient help at every stage this book would not have been possible.

"Lawyers have a superior opportunity to do good"

Abraham Lincoln

"Let's kill all the lawyers"

William Shakespeare

Preamble

HEAD2HEAD is a book about the legal profession from the perspective of an in-house lawyer.

It is based on my experiences as a Head of Legal in two major PLC's and my interviews with leading Heads of Legal Departments in some of our biggest and brightest corporations.

Why have I called it "HEAD2HEAD"?

Partly because it reflects the fact that much of the book is based on my discussions with other heads of in-house legal teams.

Mostly, however, it is because I want to challenge the profession to deliver more value.

I want the profession to deliver more value for our law firms, for the lawyers in those firms, for in-house lawyers and, above all, more value for our clients.

The book is, therefore, about going head to head against certain assumptions, perceptions and the culture and work practices of the legal profession as it is today.

Introduction

Head2Head is a book written with more than one objective in mind:

- First, it is a book about what is good and bad and indifferent about lawyers, law firms and legal services from the perspective of those of us who practice in-house.

- Secondly it is about in-house legal practice and why the in-house lawyer has become a pivotal player in the profession.

- Thirdly, and perhaps above all, it is about how we as lawyers (wherever and however we practice) can create and add value in the way we relate to our clients and each other.

It is a book that will criticise practices and working cultures that damage value as well as praising the whole profession of lawyers for its dedication and creativity on behalf of its clients. It is also about looking forward and pointing to the new opportunities for us to add value in the work that we do for our clients, our businesses and for ourselves.

For most of my career I have worked as an in-house solicitor; that is, I have been employed by (in my case two) companies to work in their own legal services departments. Only at the beginning of my career, in the early eighties, have I worked in a law firm.

I have indeed been very fortunate. Not only is being a solicitor one of the most interesting and rewarding careers anyone can have, but working as an in-house solicitor in particular is, in my opinion, the most interesting and most rewarding way to practice the law. (I use the word "rewarding" in the sense of "satisfying" rather than in the sense of the mega bucks reportedly earned by magic circle high flyers.)

To begin with, a point of detail... I am a qualified, practice certificate holding solicitor of the Supreme Court of Judicature in England and Wales (according to my admission certificate) but from now on I will use the generic term "lawyer" to describe the people I work with and those in the profession generally who are qualified to provide legal services.

In-house the distinction between solicitor, barrister, paralegal and legal executive is not so important anyway. Everyone is simply an employee of the company he or she works for and as most people in those businesses would not know (or care) about the different professional qualifications, why spend time trying to explain? Like so much in commerce and industry it is not what you call yourself that is important; it is what you do and how you do it that counts the most.

So, why is now a good time for there to be a book about lawyers and legal services from the perspective of an in-house lawyer?

To begin with this is not just a book about in-house lawyers or for in-house lawyers. Certainly it is a book that describes the phenomenon of in-house practice, but in the context of the whole profession. Above all it is about what makes outstanding lawyers and outstanding legal work, and while it recognises the success of the very many in-house lawyers who have so far achieved so much, it is also about the structural weaknesses in the profession that suggest an uncertain future for corporate legal practice in this country.

I must admit that I set out with the intention of writing a book that would record points of progress, a document to mark the maturing of a new type of lawyer. As my thoughts took shape, however, I realised there was a more important message to give.

It is that the successful management of relationships (be they within law firms, within businesses or between businesses and their lawyers) fundamentally underpins the success, profitability and longevity of those relationships.

4

The best lawyers in law firms and the best in-house lawyers are best also at relationship management and there is a great deal we can learn from them.

So, I have more than one objective in writing this book, and there are interlocking themes and issues throughout. However, if I had to say in just one sentence what I hoped to achieve, it would be this...

To show that it is within every lawyer to give a consistently outstanding service and that by managing all relationships more effectively all lawyers, whether in-house or in a law firm, can create and add value in all that they do.

SECTION ONE

The development of the in-house lawyer's role and its significance to the legal profession and to business

Introduction

It is my contention that in the last ten years the in-house sector has become the most strategically significant area of practice compared with any other sector or type of practice.

I believe there are five reasons why this has happened. In no particular order, these are that in-house lawyers:

- Lower the cost of legal services for their businesses

- Ensure greater accessibility to legal services for their businesses

- Develop a significantly better knowledge and understanding of their businesses

- Carry more influence with their businesses and are positively influenced by their businesses

- Have become expert strategic purchasers of legal services

In the next four chapters I will explore each of these issues in much more detail. By explaining and, I hope, helping to achieve a better understanding of the developing role of the in-house lawyer, I believe there are in fact significant lessons for all lawyers to learn about what corporate clients want and value.

It is a tremendous time to be a lawyer. There are so many opportunities and so much to do.

My intention throughout this book, however, is to be positive. I am very proud to be called a lawyer and I am very proud of what this profession of lawyers that I belong to achieves every single day for all the various shapes and sizes of client we act for. The fact that in this book I am sometimes critical of the way we work simply comes from a genuine desire to see the profession develop and grow.

I know that there is a huge pool of talent in the profession and I know that people in the profession work damn hard. I hope therefore that I do not make any cheap points at anyone's expense, but if I do, be sure to let me know.

Chapter One

Lower costs and greater accessibility

People are sometimes surprised at just how many lawyers now work in-house.

In October 2001 over seven thousand practising certificates were issued by the Law Society in England and Wales to solicitors working in commerce and industry.

Out of a total of 80,000 solicitors it is clear that in-house solicitors represent a significant constituency in their own right.

What the statistics do not show, however, are the total number of all lawyers working in business, or the few thousand more lawyers working in Local Government, or in the voluntary sector, or who are qualified but do not have practising certificates.

On this basis, a conservative estimate would suggest that between one in ten and one in eight lawyers work in-house.

Once deemed a home for the washed up and the burnt out, it is now for many newly qualified lawyers the first career of choice. What we are seeing is not only the fastest growing sector in the profession, but also the most strategically significant group of lawyers in the country, possibly in Europe. It is an amazing transformation and a great success story, and I will explain how shortly.

It is important to realise, however, that it was not always like this.

The Law Society Commerce & Industry Group provides the official professional banner under which the interests of in-house lawyers can be represented. It was formed in 1963. We can perhaps assume as a result that by that time in the early 1960s there was sufficient interest in the role of in-house company lawyers to warrant their own formal group.

In 1963 there were less than one thousand practising certificates issued to in-house solicitors, but more interesting than numbers is to understand how this relatively new breed of lawyer was perceived by the wider profession. It is a perception that can rear its unattractive head even today, nearly forty years on.

In-house lawyers, so the line went, were people who could not make it in the cut and thrust of a busy law firm. Worst of all, they were not able to give independent advice because they were on the payroll of their client. They were, to put it crudely, "tame" lawyers.

I doubt this was true in 1963 anymore than it is true today, but in most things in our world, perception is reality, and it was many, many years before the wider profession began to wake up to the significance and influence of in-house legal practice.

I believe the first major shift in emphasis came in the late seventies and early eighties at a time of severe economic decline in the United Kingdom.

Legal bills have never been received with great glee by anyone, anywhere at anytime. They are generally accepted as part of the pain of being in business but they are not wanted. This antipathy is obviously heightened when costs have to be cut, investment curtailed and jobs lost. If companies could spend less on lawyers, it was an obvious area to address.

The recession on this occasion, however, also coincided with an unprecedented increase in laws and regulations effecting businesses (a trend that has continued ever since despite regular but feeble attempts by successive Governments to cut red tape). Companies across the country were faced with the double whammy of increased exposure to compliance and legal risk management issues, just at the time they could least afford to pay for the legal expertise they needed.

The in-house lawyer's day had come.

Companies that had no choice but to use lawyers would routinely criticise law firms for being too expensive. The answer was obvious. It was to recruit lawyers to the company's own staff.

As a result in-house departments began to grow. Over time they would develop a role within businesses that was to become as familiar as human resources and I.T. (I have been an in-house

10

lawyer long enough to remember when HR was known as Personnel, and I.T. was about automated ledgers...a suggestion here therefore that the occasional rebranding of a role can help it develop and move on. Perhaps a point to return to later on.)

In-house lawyers do not carry the overhead of premises, do not have to make a profit and can share in the benefits of working within a major corporation in terms of facilities and technology.

In short, in-house lawyers are a lot cheaper than law firms.

Clearly, therefore, most in-house lawyers were recruited at this time on the basis that it was a cost saving exercise. Then, almost it seems to me by chance, a second significant benefit of having lawyers in-house was revealed; their accessibility.

I believe that the cost drivers were so overwhelming at the time that, even though accessibility is a very obvious advantage of being in-house, it was somewhat overlooked.

It would become, however, a very important factor indeed and has remained so ever since.

This is because, without doubt, business people value the easy access they have to legal advice when their lawyers are in the same building. Ideas can be reviewed quickly and management decisions can be verified within timeframes that suit the business. There is little or no formality, no set-piece instructions, and no jargon to have to explain. It is a benefit as significant as the cost savings gained from employing lawyers in-house, but, in my opinion, it is potentially far more valuable.

We all know the old saying about knowing the cost of everything and the value of nothing... well, accessibility is something that cannot always be costed, but its value is obvious.

Competitive advantage is a theme I will return to throughout this book, but the point can be made now. Businesses need competitive advantage to thrive. There are some very harsh realities in an economic system based on an ethos of "to the winner the spoils". Great if you are the winner... not great if you are not. Anything that can give a company an edge is extremely valuable. Easy access to quality legal advice is definitely an edge worth developing and it is often the seemingly modest advantages such as this that can make such a big difference.

In my workshops I often refer to Linford Christie winning the 100m gold medal in the 1992 Barcelona Olympics. Christie won by a small fraction of a second. Can you remember who came second? Can you remember anyone else in the race at all?

The point is that the guy who came second was capable of winning, had trained to win and might have won. If you had to measure the amount of talent he had compared to the amount of Christie's talent, could you honestly choose between them? And yet one athlete becomes a super star, the other is forgotten.

The difference on just that one day, whatever it was, amounted to Christie's competitive advantage.

The point in the context of my world is that we do not know what small matter will make my company more successful than a rival company. Sometimes we do not know whether we will be successful or not, but what we always know is that little things can make the difference. One of those little things might be speed to market, it might be realising the flaw in a plan, it might be tweaking a process that fails to comply with a regulation to one that does. In each instance accessibility to legal advice may be crucial. Accessibility helps to support competitive advantage; in-house lawyers help support competitive advantage.

So, out of a major economic recession in the early eighties, businesses employed their own legal advisers largely on grounds of cost. From cost savings however came the added value of accessibility and a strategically important added value at that.

However, the legal profession was still a bit sniffy about in-house lawyers. Valued and valuable they might be, but they should not, for example, have rights of audience and at the end of the day the feeling still persisted that "independence" was the watchword for good lawyering and in-house lawyers were not as independent as lawyers in private practice.

I do not want to labour a point that has been largely won in the last few years (in-house lawyers now have rights of audience for example), but it is worth nailing this old chestnut…if for no other reason than to allow me to get it off my chest! But in any event, there are still important opinion formers in the legal profession who do not see how anyone can be a 'proper' lawyer and work in-house. It is to them that I address the following remarks.

Reasons to be cheerful 1, 2, and 3.

Point 1. Independence of thought, intellectual rigour and an ability to argue a point of principle are not compromised by working in the same building as the client, are not compromised by being on the payroll of the client (as opposed to invoicing the client) and are not compromised by sharing in the success or failures of the client.

Independence of thought, intellectual rigour and an ability to argue a point of principle are compromised by weaknesses of approach, by failure to listen and by bad case management.

Independence is a state of mind, not a state of separation.

Point 2. Does anyone seriously believe that a major corporate undertaking in the United Kingdom employs lawyers to be able to influence and cajole those lawyers to give advice they would not be able to get from a law firm? What would be the point of that with every regulator, trading standards officer, court, consumer group and journalist being capable at some time or other of picking over every decision the company makes?

Yes, I know some will simply say 'Maxwell', but frankly the whole profession (and several other professions besides) let themselves down over the Maxwell scandal, as well as everyone else.

My point is not that things cannot go wrong, just that they are no more likely to go wrong (I would argue in fact that they are less likely to go wrong) when lawyers are in-house.

Businesses do not want tame lawyers; they want and need the best advice they can get because, as I have said, it is a competitive advantage for them.

Point 3. In America, which has an older and more developed tradition of in-house legal practice, and which tends to lead where the UK follows, in-house lawyers are an integral part of the business world.

An American corporate needs its General Counsel if it is to be confident of surviving in the cut and trust of the U.S. and global economies. So, in the biggest and most successful economy in the world and in the most litigious society in the world, in-house lawyers have a higher profile than anywhere else in the world. I do not believe they are employed for fun, I believe they are employed because they are extremely valuable to their businesses.

Time to dismount from the hobbyhorse, but let's not have any mention anymore, anywhere about a narrow definition of 'independence' being the determining factor of quality in legal advice and legal services.

Chapter Two

Business knowledge and the benefits of 'applied law'

If the growth of in-house legal practice had its beginnings in economic recession, why did it not decline (or the growth in the sector at least slow down) when the economy turned from bust to boom?

Instead the opposite is true and the in-house sector has seen significant and sustained growth, increasing in numbers year on year and becoming the fastest growing sector of the legal profession.

There are three reasons for this:

- First; all legal markets were growing and the in-house sector continued to grow with them.

- Second; law firms had not become cheaper.

- Third; in-house lawyers were able to add a third arrow to their quiver. Along side the twin benefits of cost savings and accessibility they developed a third significant advantage over lawyers in law firms: their in-depth knowledge of the businesses they worked in.

It is hard to over-estimate the significance of this last point. It is fundamental to the success of all in-house lawyers and it is what makes them uniquely qualified to serve their clients.

When recruiting lawyers into any of the teams I have managed, just about the first thing of use I have said to them (after explaining how to use the coffee machine) has been to point out that before they become high-flyers in any organisation they need to do plenty of low level reconnaissance.

Legal skills are great. They are vital and without legal skills lawyers will not succeed. It is, however, the application of those legal skills where value is created. It does not matter how clever a lawyer you are, your value will be significantly diminished if you do not understand the environment and context in which your advice will be given and received.

A well-qualified, hard working lawyer with an in-depth and detailed knowledge of his or her employer's business is a unique talent.

There will not be another lawyer in the world who can apply his or her legal skills more deftly in context, more empathetically with the goals and aspirations of his or her business, more in tune with the policies and practices of his or her company.

Wow! Talk about competitive advantage.

In-house lawyers simply cannot know too much about their businesses. But being successful is not just about acquiring knowledge of the business. Criticism of in-house lawyers in this context is that sometimes they misunderstand where to direct their influence having acquired this knowledge.

I sent a very helpful, but unsolicited, note to a senior executive and felt more than a little rebuffed when the reply to my note came from a junior clerk. Frankly, senior executives have more important things to care about. One Chief Executive Officer I worked for once told me that as "I didn't make or sell anything" he would prefer to spend more time thinking about the people who did and what they were up to. It was a fair point.

The key to success as an in-house lawyer is in knowing who makes what decisions at the various different levels of the business. When you really understand how these people work, you can begin to truly help them deal with all the stuff and nonsense that amounts to their day job; in particular helping them with the consequences of company policies, regulatory compliance and reputational risk management. It is in the practical delivery of workable solutions that an in-house lawyer's reputation is made and where value is at its most tangible.

How surprised I was as a newly recruited in-house lawyer when I realised just how much authority is often delegated to quite junior employees. The in-house lawyer needs to target his or her advice to be received by the right people at the right time and in the right way. Not advice in a vacuum, but practical, real 'pick up and use' advice that works seamlessly with the business.

Do this, and there isn't a law firm in the kingdom that will touch you for value.

Take for example a hard lesson I learnt a few years ago. The building society I worked for had a new computer system that required a revised set of loan documents and loan application forms. My job was a simple one, to draft the Data Protection Act disclaimer for one of the applications forms. This is the part of the form that says when and how personal information may be used to cross-sell to customers gym membership or a subscription to National Geographic.

I prepared a beautifully crafted clause and just in time for a particularly tight deadline. It was in plain English, clear, concise, accurate and compliant with the Act, the Registrar's guidance notes and spookily similar to a competitor's chosen words for the same purpose. I passed it on to the small co-ordinating project group that was pulling the new documents together and they gave me a resounding raspberry.

I had given them eight lines of text but they had room for only six lines on the form. They had nothing they could use. I had applied my legal skills, but added no value. I had caused delay, disruption and some anger. I had failed.

Had I known what was easy enough to know, had I related and discussed the needs of the people reliant on me with what I had to do, I would have given them what they needed. I would have been part of a team effort, contributed an important piece in the jigsaw and the result would have worked.

This is a relatively minor example, but it illustrates the point well enough. The ivory tower is no place for any lawyer to inhabit, least of all the in-house lawyer. It is a competitive world and in-house lawyers know they must deliver every bit as much as lawyers in law firms.

If anyone doubts this and still believes in-house is a more comfortable place to be, there are two points to make:

- First, in many instances law firms compete with in-house teams for the same business. There are now many examples of legal work being outsourced that was previously undertaken by in-house teams. Furthermore senior executives are very astute people. They know when advice is good and when it is not good enough. They know when they are paying too much and they know there are thousands of lawyers in the market place. Outsourcing and downsizing are every day realities.

- Second, in-house lawyers must also knuckle down to adherence to the management and performance measures that are followed by their companies; 'performance management', 'total quality management', 'key performance rewards schemes' etc. This means that in-house lawyers are being measured against the same value indicators as everyone else in their companies.

The pressure to deliver is always there. Does what you do add value? Does the way you do it add value? Does it all add up to enough value to justify keeping you? These are all questions that businesses can ask and that in-lawyers have to be able to convincingly answer.

It simply is not good enough to be an in-house lawyer (any lawyer actually) and coast along. Add value or go for in-house lawyers to add value means to know their business and consistently offer practical, commercial, usable solutions.

It really is a wonderful opportunity and privilege to be chosen as a company lawyer, to be able to influence and direct, to manage risk and supervise the development of products and policy.

It is, if you like, 'applied law' there is nothing better as a lawyer, than being at the heart of a business where legal advice is needed to help make it more successful. But with that privilege comes responsibility. In-house lawyers simply have to be close to their businesses. More than cost benefits, more than accessibility, it is where real value is not only added, it is where real value can be created too.

For me it also suggests that structurally in-house legal teams are most beneficial when they are relatively small and close to their users. It is for this reason I have also become increasingly sceptical about the value of large centralised in-house legal departments. Let me explain this further…

If I am right, then, as I have described, there are three very significant benefits to employing an in-house lawyer:

- Cost
- Accessibility
- Business knowledge

Cost is obviously important, but should not be confused with value. Access is important, but should not be confused with understanding.

Business knowledge is the clincher. It determines the quality of the advice because advice without business knowledge is merely advice from a law book. We need lawyers who can use and apply the law through their own expert filters of experience, of intuitive understanding and an appreciation of nuance. Here is value and it is here that in-house lawyers make themselves outstanding practitioners.

Large centralised services, it seems to me, are bound to sacrifice some opportunities for lawyers to get closer to their businesses for the perceived efficiencies of size. Cost, in these instances, is therefore driving the strategy and in my opinion that is a big mistake.

For a start it means putting the in-house team in the direct line of comparison with a law firm. Nothing wrong in that at face value, but why? Law firms offer something different. They have different issues to address and are needed to perform a different role.

If in-house teams are going head-to-head with law firms on cost, sooner or later the equation will become too close to call and then what? I am not averse to outsourcing (in fact later in this book I will positively encourage elements of outsourcing) but what an opportunity missed if we lose on the altar of cost both accessibility and the added value created through business knowledge. Is that not indicative of an accountancy led approach and is that not something that we, as lawyers, should have a good argument against?

As a consultant I have the privilege of working with a number of prestigious companies. I am often bowled over by the talent and dedication shown by the in-house legal teams. It is always the case, however, that the teams that are most effective, most appreciated by their business users and the teams that enjoy their work the most, are the teams that are close to their businesses.

On the other hand, every centralised service I have reviewed, while competent and hardworking, has felt remote, underused, undervalued and overworked.

This is no coincidence. The personal touch makes for good relationships; good relationships are open and sharing. Knowledge passes freely, problems are aired in the absence of recriminations, enthusiasm is passed on and it is easy to see where help is needed. A remote team, separated by more than brickwork, works in a process driven environment to deliver a commoditised service. There is a lack of empathy; emotional intelligence is replaced with a lowest common denominator approach. One size fits all.

This may be an exaggeration, but the point is a good one. In-house lawyers are capable of contributing hugely to the success of their businesses, but ONLY WHEN THEY ARE CLOSE ENOUGH.

So, cost, accessibility and business knowledge are in my judgement the three strategic influences that have shaped a new type of legal service in the last twenty years. It is a legal service that has helped transform the way the legal profession as a whole has viewed corporate clients and mostly to positive effect. The impact of the in-house lawyer, however, has been even greater than this, as we shall see in the next two chapters.

Chapter Three

Influence and what all lawyers can learn from business

We know that most in-house lawyers recruited in the early eighties were employed to save their businesses costs.

It was a straightforward matter. If it cost £10,000 in legal bills to negotiate and draft the deal to buy software, computer kit and to get it all to work properly, why not have someone in-house do that legal work and then be free to do several similar deals?

Not rocket science, just good economic common sense.

Then something amazing happened. The combined benefits of easy access to lawyers and their intimate knowledge of their businesses began to deliver a new breed of lawyer... lawyers who were commercially focused and value driven.

For the first time in the UK lawyers could make a reputation as good business people not just good lawyers.

Let us take a step back for a moment...

Lawyers have been undervalued by the business world. Actually, on reflection lawyers probably have been valued about as much as they deserved; that really means that lawyers have been underused.

Partly this is their own fault and this will be covered in later chapters, but even if we accept that lawyers have not always covered themselves in glory, they are still equipped with a fantastic set of skills and one that is perfectly matched to succeed in business.

The lawyers' skills set includes the following, and they are worth stating:

- Analytical minds
- An ability to assimilate facts quickly
- Used to dealing with changing circumstances

- Used to working to deadlines and under pressure

- Persuasive

- Good on paper

- Good on their feet

- Creative problem solvers

In fact it is hard to imagine a more appropriate list of attributes for excellence in business.

There are only two elements in the equation that are missing:

- Relationship management skills, and

- Entrepreneurial risk assessment.

If there were some way of developing lawyers to reveal these two (I perceive) missing ingredients, the world would open up to them like never before.

It should have happened already and I am sure it will happen. It is something I feel very strongly about, not least because I hate seeing unfulfilled talent and the legal profession has a long way to go to fulfil its potential.

That said, what is very interesting to see now is that in-house lawyers have already made significant inroads into this uncharted territory.

In-house lawyers are seen by many commentators, by some in private practice and by many people in business, as more commercially aware than their counterparts in law firms. Over the last three or four years I have spoken to many hundreds of lawyers from both sides of the profession and believe this to be a fair assessment.

By way of illustration (although I accept it is not proof positive) ask anyone trained in a law firm who has worked for a period on secondment with one of the firm's corporate clients about the commerciality required in-house.

I guarantee that nine out of ten will come back to the law firm with new insights into commercial priorities and how lawyers must adapt their approach to deliver value. It is not that they were not doing it or not capable of doing it before, just that being close to a business makes everyone realise how important it is to have a results orientated commercial focus.

The secondees, in nearly every case, will be better lawyers for the experience and the experience will stay with them throughout their careers.

This leads to two statements;

- First, that relationship management skills and entrepreneurialism can and should be taught, and once taught will be applied forever.

- Second, that in-house lawyers are not a different animal to their counterparts in law firms, but they clearly benefit hugely from the influence of their corporate employers.

Successful businesses are successful because they are entrepreneurial, because they have a good product and because they are good at relationship management. Bring good lawyers into close proximity with a good corporate and the result is a new breed of lawyer and one infinitely better equipped to deliver and create value.

So here is something of a revelation to everyone who thinks that law firms are destined always to be the poor relations when it comes to innovative, client focused, value-adding management techniques; in-house lawyers are NOT genetically adapted to be more commercially aware than their law firm counterparts; it is a skill they have acquired through their close association with businesses that survive and thrive on the back of their ability to deliver what their customers want.

This seems to be very significant. For a start it means there is no secret formula, no magic 'business juice', no exclusive club for executives that bars lawyers from joining.

The answer to achieving more commercial awareness and better relationship management skills lies within the grasp of the profession itself. Law firms simply need to find the people who can help them.

This is an interesting point. As we know there are thousands of law firms (about nine thousand in fact) many of whom, including some of the very biggest and best known, struggle to come to terms with how to run their own businesses.

Yet, by contrast, there are more than ten thousand in-house lawyers in this country alone who have one-to-one access to world-class I.T. talent, world-class H.R. talent, world-class CEOs, world-class F.D.s. Ten thousand in-house lawyers who have access to the latest technology, business processes, sales techniques, product-design processes, marketing and advertising techniques.

This is access and influence to die for and it is there available now, today, at this very moment, to one in ten lawyers in this country.

In-house lawyers are such a valuable commodity, for their businesses and for the whole profession. There is so much to learn from the way they work and the sooner all lawyers wake up to that fact, the better. I really do not understand why law firms have not made better use of the access to facilities that in-house lawyers enjoy.

It was stated earlier that successful businesses are successful because they 1) allied entrepreneurial talent with 2) relationship management and 3) a good product.

On this basis, law firms can certainly be said to have a potentially good product (most of the time), but scoring just one out of three on this definition of success is not a business model that excites.

If you have ever been in a partners' meeting where the issues of product, profitability and value creation were on the agenda but did not get resolved, then spare a thought for those lawyers working in your own clients' legal teams and ask yourself, "Is there something we can learn from them?"

It is unclear what the answer would be if a law firm were to ask a selection of its corporate clients for some assistance in developing a business strategy, but I am sure it is worth asking the question. After all in this age of so much talk of "partnering" between corporate clients and law firms to realise mutual benefits, is this not an ideal opportunity to test whether the arrangements can be made to be truly a two way street?

Incidentally, while we are on the point of the access and the influence that in-house lawyers have by virtue of where they work and whom they work for, they really are very lucky. Whether it is by attending corporate conferences, business meetings, or simply sharing a table in the staff canteen, there are virtually daily opportunities to be able to listen and learn from some of the most capable and talented business leaders in the world.

Hopefully it is not taken for granted. With the skills set all lawyers have, the access to amazingly talented people who have achieved great success in business should help to develop the entrepreneurial talent in the legal world that is badly needed. It will be interesting to see whether the skills are indeed developed. It is certain that there has never been a better opportunity. There is, as a result, a great responsibility on the current generation of in-house lawyers in particular to seize, challenge and break through.

Chapter Four

Purchasers of legal services

So far we have mapped out the evolution of the in-house lawyer and his or her developing role in business. We have seen how the growth in the sector had its kick-start on the back of a simple costs expedient. We have seen how through maximising the advantages of accessibility and a deep understanding of their businesses, in-house teams have become vital cogs in the corporate machine. Then, throughout the nineties new skills have developed, management skills that give in-house lawyers greater commercial awareness.

An important new role has also emerged with little or nothing to do with the law; the skilled and highly valuable role of being an expert purchaser of legal services.

It is a very unusual in-house team that can always undertake all of the legal work a business may have. In my opinion even if a legal team has that capability it is better risk management to outsource some work. To create what computer people call 'resilience', in other words not putting all your eggs in one basket!

We shall see a new opportunity for a model provision of legal services, but suffice for now to say that outsourcing is part of that model.

At the beginning of this book we noted the cost advantages of companies employing in-house lawyers but there have been many exasperated executives over the years who have questioned why, if the company has paid for in-house lawyers, it is in fact paying for them to instruct outside lawyers in law firms as well!

It would be a fair point if work that could be done and should be done by the in-house team was being routinely outsourced. Hopefully, however, that would not be the case.

What inevitably happens to all in-house legal teams is they are the first point of contact for all legal queries and related legal work. This might range from litigation when the company is being sued or wishes to sue, to employment work, to marketing and compliance roles, to transforming corporate transactions, to the CEO's son's tenancy agreement (though the last one I hope is rare indeed).

Most in-house legal teams are very small. In fact about three quarters of all in-house solicitors work in teams of no more than three. They will be geared to look after a core function, perhaps marketing, perhaps contracts, perhaps property. They will have supplementary issues to manage, such as employment, health and safety and corporate governance, but they will not have the expertise or resources to cope with either sudden influxes of unexpected work or the faintly unusual and esoteric.

It is in these circumstances that the role of expert purchaser of legal services has developed simply because it is inevitable that occasionally, and for some companies it will be routinely, external law firms are instructed.

To do this properly is both a cost saving and a value creating opportunity, particularly when you consider the different elements to the process. For example, in just about every instance where it is proposed to instruct a law firm some or all of the following issues have to be addressed:

- Selecting the right law firm for the budget

- Selecting the right experience and the right level of expertise within the right law firm

- Providing clear instructions that avoid unnecessary work

- Helping to manage the flow of information between law firm and business managers

- Interpreting advice in the context of the workplace

- Ensuring value for money by monitoring both cost and quality

- Managing the case to a timely conclusion

It is obvious that the legal team should play a crucial role in selecting and managing law firms on behalf of its company. Furthermore this does not dent in any way the cost benefit of employing an in-house lawyer. Whatever happens, the expert management of law firms under instruction is a vital cost management role. It is also potentially a cost-saving role compared with those businesses that might otherwise instruct the wrong firms at the wrong price, or be unable to implement the advice given or who perhaps simply do not understand the advice given.

I recall, for example, reviewing the Consumer Credit Act loan documents for a small provincial building society that my company had acquired in a take-over. I was very concerned that the documentation appeared not to comply with the very complicated and detailed regulations under the Act.

I was slightly reassured to be told that some time before the take-over an eminent Queen's Counsel had given emphatic advice confirming that the documents were in order. Although the QC had been instructed by a non-lawyer in the building society I was told that it was at the request of the board of directors of the building society. This obviously endowed the instructions with a level of authority and expertise that should have allayed the fears of anyone.

I may have just been unlucky in my career, but I have never yet seen any counsel, and especially not an eminent Queen's Counsel, give emphatic advice about anything. The phrase, "Well it will all depend on the judge" must be one of the most expensive and widely used pieces of advice ever given in the history of our legal system.

I therefore decided to very carefully review both the advice and the instructions.

The advice was comprehensive and very detailed. If it had been followed, the documentation, and the processes to be implemented in support of the documentation, would have been compliant. Unfortunately this was not the case.

The advice assumed that the building society's computer system would process data in a certain way. The advice assumed that account records would be kept separately. The advice assumed that technical definitions within the Act were understood by the building society.

All three assumptions were reasonable to make, all three assumptions were wrong and all three assumptions would have been challenged by a competent in-house lawyer. The subsequent dialogue between the in-house lawyer (had there been one) and the QC would have resulted in a very different set of documentation.

I do not know what the building society paid for the advice or what it cost to implement documentation that would not work. I do not know what enforcement problems may have emerged over time or what damage might have been done to the building society's reputation. What I do know is that in-house lawyers have to become expert managers of outsourced work (if they are not already experts) to ensure they add value and save costs for the companies that employ them.

What all this means is that over the last few years in-house lawyers have become the major purchasers of legal services in the United Kingdom and possibly in Europe as well not only therefore major providers of legal advice in their own right to the biggest and best companies in the country, but the major purchasers of legal services on behalf of those companies as well.

It is worth pausing for a moment at this point.

Law firms have been slow to recognise these twin roles in the past, although increasingly, and to their credit, this is changing. It remains, however, a matter of strategic importance to the whole profession and must not be underestimated in any sense. It is why I have no hesitation in describing in-house lawyers as playing a pivotal role in the future direction and success of the whole profession.

At one time I had a legal budget that ran to millions of pounds for several years. I know heads of legal departments with annual litigation budgets that alone run to eight million pounds. These are powerful people. They can make markets and they can make law firms.

One consequence of this is the ever-increasing prominence of senior in-house lawyers. This is mostly for the good but it also raises some concerns. The weekly news journals are full of profiles and commentaries about legal teams and their leaders, while news journalists want information all the time about law firm panels and panel reviews; who is off and who is on.

This higher profile is welcome and reflects the success and growth of a sector that for years was undervalued by the profession and often outrageously maligned. The risk however is a criticism I make of many law firms and it is the risk of arrogance.

After all, it is not our money that we spend. We have a role analogous to that of trustee. It is our role to spend our company's money wisely and manage the investment then made as effectively as possible. It is not our role to pontificate on the power we wield and somehow imply that the power is personal held.

I have seen and heard of beauty parades and read too many tender documents that made me cringe with embarrassment. While they fell short of asking the lawyers in law firms to enter the company's premises on their hands and knees to show the appropriate degree of respect, the exercises were still an object lesson in the abuse of a perceived dominant position.

Thankfully most in-house teams are not like this and, as we should all realise, the most successful relationships are successful because each party's interests can be satisfied to a large degree. The interests of the company are paramount, but the interests of the law firm have also to be judged appropriately. It is inappropriate in my judgement to screw law firms into the ground.

All that said, I think on balance the in-house lawyer's role has developed with remarkable success. The consequent competitive forces that have been rejuvenated as a result are undoubtedly a good thing.

Law firms are now more competitive on service; though they over-price themselves far too often and lose potentially very profitably work as a result. Law firms, however, are more attuned to value-adding initiatives and the standards of client care in the corporate sector have risen noticeably.

Much of this improvement can be attributed to the expert selection, instruction and management of law firms by in-house lawyers and I for one welcome that influence.

Ask me however whether law firms offer enough value, if they always have the right appreciation of commercial imperatives and whether they have a clear understanding of where value truly lies, and I will be less enthusiastic. Law firms have a long road to travel before they arrive at that particular destination…At least however they are on the road, and good luck to them.

…The not always very magical magic circle

The next few paragraphs may be a little unfair. Yet nearly all law firms are guilty at some point of the failings I describe. I want to make the points because the self styled magic circle of five or six of the biggest City law businesses make such huge sums of money from their corporate clients. When so much money can be made, the level of scrutiny really should be higher than it is. I therefore make no apology for singling out the magic circle for particular comment.

The arena of the corporate takeover is perhaps the one significant area of legal work where in-house lawyers tend not to select and give the initial instruction to the law firm.

In this environment it is the merchant banks that hold sway. They have the power of conferment in some of the most lucrative deals anywhere in the world and it is the magic circle firms who are the key beneficiaries.

Go into most boardrooms and the directors there will hold the senior in-house lawyer in the highest regard, but he or she will not have a place at the board table. This is, in my opinion, one of the structural weaknesses that should be addressed if even more value is to be created for companies and their lawyers. It is another matter I will come to in detail later.

The issue in this context, however, is that the absence of a senior lawyer in our major corporations who is also a board director has meant that magic circle firms have to a large extent avoided the same rigour of selection that has been applied to most other law firms used by in-house lawyers in recent years.

The result, not to put too fine a point on it, is a self-serving club that sees merchant banks consistently selecting a very few favoured law firms to act on behalf of their corporate clients.

The boardroom in a takeover situation is a tense place to be. The merchant banks are the key advisers and the directors' security blanket. The directors are under the closest spotlight, decisions are scrutinised and policy dictated by more outside influences than at any other time.

Frankly, and probably understandably, it is not a time when directors are necessarily prepared to listen to an in-house lawyer explain why one law firm should not be used in favour of another. It is simply not something that they will feel should appear on their radar screens as an issue. Crucially the directors will not see any reason to challenge the expensive advice of their chosen merchant bank on what is for them a very low priority matter.

No one ever got sacked for choosing IBM is an old adage that comes to my mind when magic circle firms are used in corporate take-overs.

So, fat fees for the banks, fat fees for the accountants and fat fees for the very few lawyers involved. It also means a virtual lockout of the majority of perfectly expert and competent national, regional and 'non-circle' City law firms. Ironically it is these firms that have done most in the last five years to develop strategies for service and value. I hope they are able to break through.

All this helps to explain why so many senior in-house lawyers really prefer not to use the so called magic circle law firms and would be more content to use the less mysterious majority of firms they have come to respect and trust.

This is not to be overly critical of these major players in the global marketplace. Their work, on occasions, reaches the heights of brilliance, their earning potential is amazing and the resources at their disposal are great indeed.

These are all reasons to celebrate their success and given that the profession is not always awash with good news stories, in some ways it seems churlish to carp.

My particular perspective, however, is driven by a wish to see even the most obviously successful parts of our profession improve standards of service and, particularly, value, so that they become even more successful and important.

Not all the magic circle firms are consistently good at all the work they do for all of their clients. Too often they ride on the back of their reputations and rely overmuch on the weight carried by their esteemed letterheads.

This is not to suggest that their work is not of a very high order, but occasionally there is, for example, a lack of control over which lawyers within the firm are incurring chargeable time. Sometimes there is a lack of co-ordination of the outputs as well. A further common criticism is the maelstrom of activity at the end of a deal that is terribly hard for the client to either manage or argue with in any realistic way. Inevitably costs also race away as a deal closes and there is nearly always a lack of transparency as to precisely what is going on.

It is inescapable that the quality of lawyers in these huge law firms can be variable. Business clients rarely need the rocket scientists, so it is entirely appropriate to have files managed by lawyers that do not need oxygen to be able to breathe. This, however, is rarely reflected in the fees that are charged. When top dollar is paid, expectations are highest; those expectations are not always met.

Finally it is also sometimes the case that the house style dictates that the client's preferences have to bend to the will of the law firm and not the other way round and too often the client is left as a spectator to a deal and is not treated as a participant.

Not all this will always be the fault of the law firm, but the lack of selection scrutiny is partly to blame because it has allowed the firms to concentrate on things other than their relationship skills. I think this may be one chicken yet to come home to roost, but if and when it ever finds the coop, the fallout may be very interesting indeed.

...In summary

What is clear is that through the last five years the selection, instruction and management of law firms by in-house lawyers on behalf of their companies has been a significant development in the role of the in-house lawyer.

Speaking to employers who do not have an in-house lawyer I have sought to persuade them that even if they thought they would still use their friendly law firms, the closer management of those firms for value and quality would by itself pay for the in-house overhead. They would then have the newly recruited in-house lawyer also available to do some legal work themselves at no real cost to the business.

The in-house lawyer as manager of legal services is of benefit and relevance to the whole profession and to corporations. It has become a vital role and in-house lawyers need to be sure themselves that they have the skills, expertise and market knowledge to add value.

In-house lawyers are significant in terms of their sheer weight of numbers, the value and competitive advantage they give their employing companies, the development of new skills and commercial awareness and their purchasing influence across the whole profession.

The sector has come an awful long way since the Law Society Commerce & Industry Group was formed in 1963. Mostly the contribution has been positive. The legal profession and businesses in this country are better for the influence of in-house legal advice. It is, however, something we now need to develop even further to bring about more competition, better levels of expertise, the highest levels of service and even more value for clients.

SECTION TWO

Relationship management and the road to value creation

Introduction

The first section of this book described the developing role of the in-house sector from the 1960s to the present day. The sector is significant in many ways but perhaps of most importance is the pivotal role it plays as both provider and purchaser of legal services. This places the sector uniquely within the sphere of influence of the business world and the world of the law firms.

As already described, there are many lessons that the legal profession can and should learn from a close association with business. The second section of the book draws on this pivotal role held by the in-house sector to describe what is the single most important lesson the whole legal profession can learn from the business world: relationship management.

Chapter Five

Perception is reality

One thing that becomes obvious when talking to lawyers is that most of them really enjoy their legal work. They enjoy the nitty-gritty of working through problems and finding solutions. They like the complexity, the history and the mystique associated with the law. They like the intellectual challenge of having an opponent to argue against and they enjoy winning.

Talk to these lawyers about aspects of their work they dislike and many will say simply 'marketing'. By this they do not mean trying to come up with some scintillating strap lines for a television advertising campaign. What they mean is promoting themselves, their firm, their product, and their colleagues. They mean relating to clients and potential clients. They mean, in short, everything apart from the legal work.

This is the brutal truth for thousands of lawyers. They get their kicks from the black letter stuff and really do not want much to do, to put it bluntly, with the people stuff.

This presents a significant problem because sadly for these lawyers it is the people stuff that pays the bills.

Many people reading this will have heard of Pareto and the 80:20 rule. I am not a scientist and do not know whether the 80:20 rule is a 'rule' or just a neat observation that can be applied 'as a rule'. The point, however, is that typically lawyers perceive that they split their working day between legal work 80% and people work 20%, when actually, in my view, the focus should be the other way around with legal work at 20% and people work at 80%.

This perceived misalignment is a significant reason why law firms miss opportunities to be more profitable and to add value for their corporate clients. It is also a reason why some in-house teams have lost their way a little in concentrating too much on processing legal work and not enough on building their understanding of their companies and the relationships within their companies.

I have devised a *perception test* to illustrate the differences of understanding between client and lawyer in relation to qualities of service.

It is very simply, as you can see below, twenty paired statements where the intention is that one statement in the pair has to be favoured over the other. In the test no qualified choices can be made; a definite choice between the two statements is required on each occasion.

The perception test

The paired statements should be, depending on the context, preceded with;

'Which do you prefer/admire the most',

'value the most' or

'consider to be more important'

Remember also that the test is not meant to be empirically proven; it is about perceptions.

Why not try the perception test yourself before you read my analysis.

You may even want to try the test on your colleagues and clients as well. I am sure that understanding their perceptions of your service will be helpful to you whether or not the results of your tests strike a chord with my conclusions.

The twenty paired statements are set out on the next page and are followed by an analysis of the results from tests I have undertaken in the course of my research for this book:

1 a. Legal skills or b. People skills

2 a. Speed of response or b. Accuracy of response

3 a. Pragmatism or b. Compliance

4 a. Helpfulness or b. The right answer

5 a. Brand values or b. Independent approach

6	a. Internal legal team or b. External law firm
7	a. Working with the business or b. Challenging of the business
8	a. Working beyond the brief or b. Working within the brief
9	a. Build relationships or b. Be reactive
10.	a. Team player or b. Impartial neutral
11	a. Be creative or b. Be secure
12	a. Reliable and timely or b. Innovative but late
13	a. Competitive advantage or b. Whiter than white
14	a. Persuasive or b. Collaborative
15	a. Service standards or b. Enthusiasm
16	a. Cheerful or b. Healthy cynicism
17	a. Professionalism or b. Mucking-in
18	a. Sharing goals or b. An appropriate filter for bad ideas
19	a. Ensuring the business is protected or b. Ensuring the business is successful
20	a. Delivery or b. Content

The disclaimer!

Before looking at the test results I want to make clear that this is not a scientific survey. Questions are not calibrated to elicit a verifiable response against a test database, nor is there a sufficiently large sample for the results to be statistically significant.

What I have done is to pose some typical daily conundrums faced by lawyers and their clients to reasonably representative groups and then considered what their responses revealed about the quality of relationship management by the lawyers.

The sample

Over a period of nine months forty-eight in-house lawyers were interviewed either as part of the consultancy work I was engaged in at the time or in research for this book. Similarly I interviewed twenty-five lawyers in law firms and twenty-five senior managers in business in various large companies who were used to working with lawyers.

From such a small sample the results are not capable of being extrapolated across the whole profession, but they are illustrative of attitudes and perceptions. I think they are revealing and I would be confident that a more comprehensive survey would show similar results.

The results

1. Legal skills or people skills?

Seventy five percent of the business people surveyed preferred people skills to legal skills.Twenty five percent of lawyers in law firms, however, valued people skills more highly than legal skills. Sixty percent of in-house lawyers favoured people skills over legal skills.

The entirely opposite views held by lawyers in law firms and by the business managers on the relative importance of people skills and legal skills are pertinent.

It seems to highlight one of the more significant relationship issues between lawyers and clients and one good reason for writing this book.

When a corporate client instructs a law firm, it does not doubt that the law firm can do the legal work. The company does not have any comprehension at all that a particular legal expertise will be beyond the wit of any firm of lawyers. All corporate clients make the assumption that their lawyers will not fail because of a lack of knowledge of the law.

Furthermore, while a client might suspect that a big law firm will charge more than a small law firm, it will have no real notion of comparative value in the legal expertise of the different law firms.

What the client is able to judge, and what it will understand very well, is a sense of service, of care, of communication and of empathy. As the client is able to make a judgement in respect of these things, it is also much more likely to attribute a sense of value in respect of them. At the end of the day a company simply wants to be made to feel important however mundane the problem may be.

This is common sense, but it is commonly absent in many law firms. What we see in the answers to this one question is that law firms have no real appreciation what their customers are likely to value. If anything the law firms are more likely to value legal expertise and this is the very thing their corporate clients are unable to value particularly highly.

We also see that in-house lawyers, who are obviously physically (at least) closer to their clients, are much more in tune with this perception, although they too need to close the gap somewhat.

Clearly all lawyers need to understand this point much better than they appear to understand it at present. No one would claim that legal expertise was unimportant (very often it is obviously essential). The point however is that, when judging value and the effectiveness of the service a law firm has given, corporate clients are very often assessing different qualities to those valued by the law firm.

2. Speed of response or accuracy of response?

Sixty percent of business people preferred speed of response to the accuracy of the response. Forty percent of lawyers in law firms favoured speed of response. Fifty percent of in-house lawyers preferred speed and fifty percent preferred accuracy.

I do not think that this means that corporate clients want wrong answers given more quickly.

We all realise that time is a precious commodity and that speed is capable of assuming the characteristic of a competitive advantage. An answer or a solution that is usable, but not honed and polished, is probably more valuable in many instances, if it can be delivered more quickly than the well-crafted, well-presented report that follows a day or so later.

We are all guilty sometimes of wanting to make the right impression with a client by thinking that presentation was the paramount consideration. In fact, in most cases, presentation counts for relatively little. The key to many successful outcomes is speed of response.

The irony in this conclusion is that many businesses might actually be prepared to pay lawyers a premium for a usable solution that is given more quickly and yet the legal profession is largely tied, even today, to charging for its services by reference to the length of time it takes to do the work.

Isn't that an interesting problem to pose the creative problem solving profession?

3 & 4. Pragmatism or compliance, and helpfulness or the right answer?

Questions 3 and 4 present a similar picture.

Most business people questioned favoured pragmatism over compliance and valued helpfulness more highly than always getting the right answer. Interestingly in-house lawyers also favoured pragmatism over compliance but lawyers in law firms felt that compliance was more important.

It is perhaps unfair to read too much into this. Law firms cannot easily turn round to their clients and say, "You'll be breaking the law, but what the heck".

What most law firms already realise, however, is that in many instances compliance is not a black and white decision. There are very often shades of grey and therefore room for some interpretation. Where there is room for interpretation there is also room for competitive advantage. Lawyers who find the room for manoeuvre are the lawyers who add most value because they find competitive advantage for their clients.

Not just valuable, but potentially invaluable.

In these instances the clear signal from clients is that they want their lawyers to come off the fence and perhaps even to share in some of the risk with them.

These days there is much talk of 'partnering' arrangements between law firms and their corporate clients, but there will never be a true partnering relationship until law firms are genuinely able to share some of the risk with their clients.

Valuing helpfulness over the right answer echoes the points made earlier about speed of response being more important than the accuracy of the response.

In my experience law firms do not get this at all. How can it be that you can be wrong and be helpful at the same time? The truth, of course, is that clients expect to get a right answer in any and all cases, but what they want most of all is the most helpful right answer.

This goes back to my story about the data protection clause. My eight lines of text was a correct answer, but it was not a helpful answer. If lawyers persist in giving correct answers without understanding how helpful those answers will be in context, they should not be surprised to find that their clients are not always so enamoured of their work.

5. Brand values or independent thought?

Question 5 needs a little more explanation.

Brand values are key to a company's success. To succeed at any level, businesses need to have a good product, be well managed and well led. Leadership is about espousing a vision that is credible, achievable and understood and appreciated by most of the people who have to work with it.

In my experience it is always reassuring for business people (and highly valued by them) if the brand values of their company are accepted by their lawyers. The conflict with this concept that can sometimes arise is the natural resistance of lawyers to becoming too closely associated with their client. This in turn becomes a question of the lawyer's independence.

As we saw earlier, independence is something lawyers hang on to as if it were holy writ handed down through the generations.

The difficulty lawyers have with this issue is understandable. The independence of the judiciary is clearly appreciated and valued. It is also clear that independent thinking is crucial to the success and integrity of all lawyers. Obviously lawyers must never concede ground to opinions they believe would be professionally compromising.

We must not accept the attitude that says lawyers should not get so close to a client so as to feel the pressure the client feels or to see the impact of circumstance.

Such attitudes are wrong and in my opinion the closer a lawyer can get to the heart of the matter, the better. Advice should never be given in a vacuum. Businesses want their lawyers (in-house or in law firms) to be part of their team and to see the problems from the point of view of the business.

What distinguishes merely a good lawyer in this area from an outstanding lawyer is the ability of the outstanding lawyer to get so close to a client that he or she becomes a trusted team player; yet he or she remains able to retain the independence of thought to give useful, sometimes difficult, advice when the situation demands.

In my survey both in-house lawyers and lawyers in law firms valued independence above brand values. All the business people surveyed, however, thought that brand values were more important.

By itself this tells us very little except that in terms of the client's perception the lawyers are giving them a different message to the one they might want to receive.

Independence is, after all, perhaps only a short step away from being seen to be aloof, arrogant and uncaring. It would be very unfortunate if lawyers' proper regard for ensuring the right degree of independence was confused with arrogance.

All are advised to be careful. Independence is not necessarily a concept the client will always appreciate or that can be easily conveyed.

6. In-house team or law firm?

Question 6 is about preferring to work with in-house lawyers or law firms.

Not surprisingly the majority of business people asked said they would prefer to work with their in-house team.

This is not a meaningless response even though it may appear to be an obvious response.

The question to ask is, "Do business people think that in-house lawyers are better lawyers?"

Most emphatically they do not.

In fact nearly everyone I have ever worked with assumed that lawyers in law firms were better lawyers than the lawyers in-house simply because the law firms were more expensive and the lawyers there tended to be paid more than in-house lawyers!

So if business people do not think that their in-house lawyers are better lawyers (if, in fact, they tend to think that law firms have the better lawyers), why do they prefer to use the in-house team?

It is because the in-house team is perceived to be a known quantity, commercially minded, accessible, committed and on the same side.

Being successful, in this context, is therefore not about having better legal skills or more in-depth resources; it is about better relationships.

The more that law firms understand this potential mindset of their clients the better they will respond to their clients' wishes and the better service they will provide. It then follows that the better the service the more appreciative and loyal the client will be and the more loyal the client the more profitable will be the relationship.

7. Working with the business or challenging of the business?

In the survey the client, the in-house lawyers and the lawyers with law firms collectively agreed that the role of the lawyer was to work with the business client.

This had a one hundred percent response from the client managers, a ninety percent response from in-house lawyers and an eighty percent response from the lawyers with law firms.

This is broadly in line with what one might expect.

The only point to make is that the business people interviewed would not understand any response that even hinted at their lawyers not working with them. In a world where we know that perception is reality great care is needed to be seen to support the client's view.

While lawyers sometimes have to wear different hats and always retain their independence of judgement, there is still, I think, a concern in these results. For between ten and twenty percent of lawyers to be perceived by their clients as not working with them is a significant credibility gap to close.

The response may be right, but like the concept of independence it is a tough one to sell.

8. Work beyond the brief or work within the brief?

Unanimity!

Everyone agrees that all lawyers should work beyond the brief.

However, how many clients believe that their lawyers actually work beyond the brief? Do they think that their lawyers are genuinely striving to add value and are not just undertaking a task according to a tried and trusted process?

Nearly every lawyer works beyond the brief.

Lawyers are some of the most dedicated and hard working professionals in any field in any arena. Their enthusiasm for their subject and their willingness to take on more work if it supports the client is obvious.

My in-house teams often seemed to have an infinite capacity to take on new work and they never proved me wrong. Not one of the team ever refused to help when a particular problem arose.

However, most clients are completely and blissfully unaware of the superb efforts made in their name and on their behalf. How sad is that?

As an issue, this comes under the heading of 'communication'.

The point is that if the lawyer is doing more, adding more, making a process easier, helping things run more smoothly, discovering the tangential problems and then solving them, the lawyer should not be surprised if the client does not notice. The lawyer must explain, repeat and state it again!

If you are being brilliant, then for goodness sake make sure that you tell the person on whose behalf you are shining so brightly!

This really is a major point, particularly for law firms. We have seen from the answers to the first question that clients do not necessarily understand how to value (or compare) legal expertise.

A brilliant job well done or a simple job botched can appear to be handled in the same way. Lawyers have got to make their work more accessible to the layman. Accessibility and transparency will lead to greater understanding and understanding will lead to more appreciation. When that happens, billing for value becomes a possibility and, in my opinion, billing for value will be far more profitable than billing for time.

For as long as lawyers wrap their work in a cloak of bewigged mystique, clients will at best fail to see value and at worst mistrust that value for them was ever there at all.

9. Building relationships or being reactive?

More unanimity.

Everyone agrees that it is better to build relationships.

If only people did what they said they thought they should do.

At a weekend conference law firms had an opportunity to meet with selected in-house lawyers with whom they had not previously had a lawyer-client relationship and, to put it at its most basic, do what might be called a "cold pitch" for work.

Here was an entirely artificial environment where everyone felt a little uncomfortable, so the job of the law firm, in my opinion, was to try and build some rapport with the prospective client. What actually happened (time and time again I might add) was that the law firms simply told the in-house lawyers how good they were at doing particular types of legal work.

As we have seen before, in-house lawyers tend to know that law firms are good at doing legal work; most after all were recruited from law firms in the first place!

What the in-house lawyers would like to know, however, is whether the particular law firm can work with the particular client and make the relationship worth the effort. The primary source of information for the law firm is therefore not itself, but the client.

If the law firm's representatives could not ask a single open question in a half hour interview, if they could not find out one new piece of information, if they could not adapt their script to any extent at all, how the hell would they build a relationship?

This is a major skills deficit in lawyers and one that badly needs to be addressed. At the moment we seem to work in a world where many lawyers have little or no idea how to present their 'product' to a prospective client. It is the equivalent of keeping the shutters down on a shop front and it is not very welcoming.

10. Team player or impartial neutral?

The answers to this question mirrored those to question 5.

The client wants team players. The client does not understand that there may be another role to fulfil. Lawyers should at least maintain the perception that they are team players even when they are thinking independently because it clearly makes the client feel more comfortable.

A comfortable client is a client who will stick with their lawyer through thick and thin. Such a client is called an asset and I tend to the old fashioned view that assets are generally worth having.

11. Creative or secure?

This question throws up a neat conundrum for the business clients rather than the lawyers.

Do these businesses want to work in the safe ground, where their creativity has a firmer foundation, or do they want to shift to the less secure ground where the rewards may be higher but where their own creativity also carries more risk?

Much will, of course, depend on the nature of the legal issues at stake. What this book will seek to demonstrate later is that good relationships allow for more risk and more creativity. Less stable relationships force a move towards a more conservative approach.

It is very hard to give very creative solutions if the relationship with the client is not good. It is equally hard for a client to accept more risk when it has some reservations about the lawyers. It is also the case however that the more creative a solution can be the more valuable it becomes. Here again profitability and value has a direct link to the quality of the relationship.

Business managers were evenly split on this one. In-house lawyers favoured creativity as did law firms though by a smaller majority.

Perhaps the lesson here is that creativity is a good thing, but only if the client has sufficient trust in the relationship.

12. Reliable and timely or innovative but late?

Another tricky question for the business managers.

Again they were evenly split. In-house lawyers felt that reliable and timely was better as did lawyers from law firms, although in their case by a more significant margin.

This is also about relationships. When relationships are being established, the important objectives are to be timely, relevant and helpful. Invention is great, but until the relationship is established how can any lawyer be sure if invention is needed, wanted or relevant?

Clever solutions can be misunderstood as an attempt to raise the level of fees or to 'show-off' and neither is an endearing trait.

Later in the relationship when needs are fully understood and some room for manoeuvre is available, invention may demonstrate added value and commitment.

What is absolutely key therefore is to appreciate how the client wants his or her affairs to be managed. To offer a house style approach where 'one size fits all' is to risk sending a signal that says the law firm is more important than the client.

Lawyers must learn to listen as well as talk.

13. Competitive advantage or whiter than white?

I can vividly remember a meeting to discuss how to implement a new code of practice for selling financial services and being told that my advice was forcing the company to be 'whiter than white'.

It was not said as a compliment and I did not take it as such.

Businesses want to comply with the law because they do not want to risk the hard won reputation of their brand. However ask company directors whether they like the number of laws and regulations that affect the business and they will say they do not. Ask directors if they would therefore like to make a stand against over-regulation by ignoring the same legislation and they will think you have gone mad. Of course the belief is that they should comply.

What they do not want, however, is to be 'whiter than white', overburdened with compliance and so be a step behind their competitors as a result.

Lawyers who do not understand this point will disappoint their clients.

Furthermore lawyers who understand the point, but who do not understand their clients sufficiently well will not be able to give advice that can exploit competitive advantage and still allow the company to be compliant with the law.

In both instances it is about relationships and building understanding. In the meeting where I was accused of being 'whiter than white' it was, of course, a gross injustice to me (although my maturing years now allow me to look back without bitterness) but where I could be criticised legitimately was in failing to communicate just how significant this new code of practice was going to be and therefore how significant the impact might be on the sales processes. Communication, as already mentioned, is therefore a vital area and will be covered in much more detail later.

In terms of the survey 100% of managers wanted advice that might give them a competitive advantage. The amazing thing to me was that less than 100% of lawyers wanted to give their clients advice that would give them a competitive advantage.

What sort of a signal is that?

Again it may be a misunderstanding of roles or just a cautious reply born of some less than satisfactory experience. It is important however (and I know I am repeating myself, but the point is crucial) to realise how the attitude of the lawyer is interpreted by the client.

It is not that the lawyer is wrong in any sense except one. The lawyer has not allowed for the client's perception to govern the actions and attitudes of the lawyer. The risk is that the client will not see or understand what was actually intended and opportunities to add value may be diminished or even lost altogether.

14. Persuasive or collaborative?

Another tricky question.

As an in-house lawyer I was most effective when the people I was trying to persuade believed that they had had the same idea as me before I said what I was thinking!

It is a truism, but no one likes a clever Dick. If the clever Dick is a lawyer, the problem is compounded.

Remember that CEO who told me that, as I did not make or sell anything, I was less important than the people in his organisation who did make and sell things. Lawyers want and need to be persuasive. It is what we are trained to do after all. Business people on the other hand do not want to be persuaded. What they want is for us to help them do their jobs better (and to help them get the glory).

Not surprisingly a significant majority of business people wanted collaborative lawyers, while law firm lawyers had a similar majority favouring a persuasive approach.

The result is two sets of people who want the exact same thing, but who have a perception deficit over that reality.

A refocusing by law firms would not result in a significantly different approach, but it just might lead to a different perception and significantly better relationships as a result.

This is a point worth dwelling on. Nearly everything said so far would not cost the law firm (or the in-house legal team) a single penny to implement.

There are no hordes of management consultants crawling disruptively over every aspect of the business (although I am available in a very non-disruptive way at a very modest cost!). No luvvies with strange hair and improbable suits advising on brand and marketing. No expensive hospitality or sponsorship involved.

Yet I believe the issues highlighted are capable of creating better, more valuable and longer lasting client relationships. Cheap at half the price!

15. Service standards or enthusiasm?

One of the phrases that is bandied around by HR professionals in their performance management programmes is 'service standards'.

By this is meant the expected level of service for a given task or process. The aim is to document a checklist for managers to be able to confirm that minimum service levels have been attained. In other words, ticks can be put in the relevant boxes.

What sometimes happens is that service standards become the means by which less than outstanding help and co-operation can be given. Service standards actually permit average performances.

In my opinion this is one of the deficiencies of having too structured a management process, as it tends to discourage individual flair and creativity.

I may come across as an advocate for bringing modern management techniques to lawyers; although that's true, I do not believe that the unique attributes of lawyers need to be totally subjugated to processes and checklists.

Within all lawyers I believe there is a streak of individualism. Service standards may have their place, but please not at the expense of creative problem solving or the application of emotional intelligence.

The survey showed that business managers favoured service standards, but that both in-house lawyers and lawyers from law firms on balance preferred enthusiasm.

Service standards need to be in place for the administration issues in the client-lawyer relationship, such as returning phone calls and answering correspondence, billing intervals, review meetings etc, but there should not be fixed service standards relating to the outputs of the creative process.

We are still a profession after all and minimum professional standards should not need to be spelt out, and should be of the highest order in any event.

Lawyers must also have the opportunity and be encouraged to deliver excellence. I for one tend to think that service standards in this context have the affect of lowering expectations of excellence when we should be raising expectations of excellence instead.

16. Cheerful or healthy cynicism?

Among themselves lawyers often swap their war stories in wearied tones of how such-and-such an issue came up again for the umpteenth time or how so-and-so in marketing/sales tried it on again.

These are the bonding stories, the stories that allow lawyers to empathise and sympathise with each other during or following stressful situations.

The, so-called, healthy cynicism this engenders, however, must not spill over into the relationship with the client.

Healthy cynicism is a difficult emotion to convey. It is, as a result, an emotion that is open to a number of unintended interpretations. Your client may mistake your ironic and amusing comments for arrogance, or being uncooperative, or sounding miserable. You may find inadvertently that clients become wary and distrusting of your credentials as a team player.

Always be cheerful with your clients and keep your cynicism (healthy or otherwise) for the bar and a drink with your lawyer chums.

In the survey 100% of managers preferred people to be cheerful. Of the 5% of lawyers who thought that their healthy cynicism was a better approach, please think again.

As a young newly qualified lawyer I was often told that lawyers come with baggage. It says, "I am cleverer than you", "I am very expensive" and, "I do not have to smile a lot to do my job". Many clients cope with this and give back their well-worn lawyer jokes with boring regularity. The point is though that if you are a little bit nervous, unsure or just inexperienced, dealing with lawyers can be an ordeal.

So smile. It helps such a lot. Be a good guy, even if you are pretending!

17. Professionalism or mucking-in?

This question raises similar points to the last question.

Lawyers instinctively believe that their professionalism is a credit to them and they are right, but only to a point. The point here is not whether lawyers should be unprofessional, but how their clients might sometimes perceive their professionalism.

As just mentioned, there is so much baggage that comes with the law. Perceptions are that lawyers are fabulously and undeservedly well paid, that they tend to over-complicate matters, that they force otherwise amicable people to fight each other, that they prolong and procrastinate and are generally self-serving.

The risk in promoting 'professionalism' is that it has the same cachet as the 'professional foul' in soccer. In addition in many cases business people will misconstrue professionalism as meaning a lack of commercialism. For both reasons, care is needed.

The smarter approach is to maintain the highest ethical and professional standards in your work, but do so as a matter of course and in the background. Then go about dispelling some of the myths that surround lawyers and roll up your sleeves to help your client with the particular problems he or she faces.

In the survey a majority of business managers preferred a less stuffy approach (their interpretation of professionalism) while a majority of lawyers, including the in-house lawyers favoured professionalism.

It is another small example of how perception is reality and it is the clients' perceptions that we have to address, not our own.

18. Sharing goals or an appropriate filter for bad ideas?

More now on a familiar theme.

Sometimes we have to give bad news. We have to step aside from the team and say unpalatable things. On due reflection we have come to the conclusion that for a particular product, project or case, there is no quick solution, there is no cost free

59

solution, or simply that there is no solution (quick, cost free or otherwise).

Directors in their boardrooms want their lawyers to perform this role. Directors expect their in-house lawyers or the law firms that are engaged on behalf of their companies to make sure that the line of non-compliance is not crossed. It is the safety net role and it is vital in any corporate governance regime.

The managers and staff with whom the lawyers are working day to day on projects, however, have less sympathy with this particular aspect of a lawyer's job. They have a target or an objective to reach. They may have some personal stake in the outcome (a possible promotion perhaps; certainly their reputation will be at stake) and the last thing they want to hear is the news that a problem has blocked progress or killed the project altogether.

Having to wear different hats at the same time is what makes the job of a lawyer both fascinating and difficult.

In truth the lawyer should be able both to share goals with commitment and enthusiasm and also to stand back from the fray and determine when he or she needs to sound the alarm bell.

The concern is not that lawyers do not realise that this is their role, but that they are not well enough equipped to communicate and relate to their clients on this basis.

In the survey the business managers all preferred their lawyers to share their goals. The in-house lawyers were evenly split but with a slight majority in favour of sharing goals. Lawyers in the law firms said, by a similarly small majority, that their role was as a filter for bad ideas.

We can be comfortable with this result. It reflects the slightly different roles that the in-house lawyer and the law firm should adopt. These different roles will be explored in more detail later.

19. Ensuring the business is protected or ensuring the business is successful?

Lawyers sometimes become too preoccupied with making sure the safety net is fully secure and do not give enough time applying their creative skills to maximising opportunity for successful outcomes.

In many businesses the regulatory regime can appear suffocating. It is tempting for the lawyers to appear almost to relish the power they wield to apparently block and obstruct ideas that will allow their business to develop and compete.

This is only a perception. Lawyers actually dislike blocking good ideas as much as the managers dislike their ideas being blocked. The perception, nevertheless, needs to be addressed.

In the survey all the business managers wanted their lawyers to help their companies to become more successful. The lawyers, however, had a split focus and, while most wanted the companies to be successful, a significant minority thought their more valuable role was to ensure that their clients were protected.

It is hard to argue that they might be wrong, but this analysis is not about rights and wrongs; it is about perceptions.

Lawyers have tremendous creative talents and a training background that facilitates the opportunity for them to find creative solutions. It is, however, possible to perceive the repeated blocking of new ideas on whatever grounds as failing to apply those creative talents more positively. On occasions lawyers take the easy (lazy) option of presenting a negative stance to new proposals instead of engaging with the business people in a creative exercise to see what might be done after all.

This may be a misconception but if the perception created by a particular approach is that the lawyer is not working always for the positive interests of the business, then that is a perception that cannot be ignored.

All lawyers need to be aware of how their clients may perceive perfectly correct and legitimate positions and ensure that those perceptions are not negatively skewed against the lawyers.

20. Content or delivery?

The last question in the perception test is designed to show the main point of the whole exercise.

Both the content of a piece of work and how that work is delivered to the client are of great significance. If you had to choose between the two, to say what was the most important, what would you say?

In the survey eighty percent of business managers said that delivery was more important than content. In-house lawyers agreed with sixty percent believing that delivery was more important than content as well. The lawyers in law firms however had a different perception; sixty percent of them felt that content was more important than delivery.

Again we are not talking about fundamental issues illustrating profound structural weakness. What we are observing is that lawyers and clients sometimes have different objectives.

The closer the lawyers can get to understanding their clients' objectives, the better the service they will offer. An improved service is likely to be used more often and may even carry a premium rate of charge.

The client is happy, the law firm is happy the individual lawyers involved are happier too. Is that not a result worth striving for?

In the circumstances of whether delivery is more important than content, we are obviously not considering that the content can be wrong. What we are noting is a matter of commercial pragmatism.

Businesses need advice they can use. Usable advice is targeted, timely and relevant. The style of delivery, the timing of delivery and to whom the advice is delivered are genuinely more likely to be more important to a business manager than whether every last point has been addressed, whether the report fits the house style of the law firm or whether the report will pass scrutiny by the firms P.I. insurers.

The law firm is not wrong, client care service standards may have been fully met, and the bill may even be paid on time. But has the firm exploited every opportunity to add and create value? Has the service been genuinely in tune with the client's needs? Has the client concluded that he or she would relish another opportunity to work with the law firm again?

When these issues can be answered positively by both lawyer and client, the service will have been truly outstanding. And every one of us is capable of doing it.

Conclusions

This survey was not a scientific exercise. You may in fact disagree fundamentally with the analysis, but what is incontrovertible is that we are all sometimes guilty of failing to notice the clients' perspectives or to have sufficient regard to how our actions may be interpreted.

You may also have noticed that the analysis of the perception test began with a disclaimer. I wrote that it was not a statistically significant sample, but that nevertheless I trusted the results. How many of you thought, when you read that statement, "So what's the point of your analysis"? How many of you subsequently felt more inclined to disagree with my conclusions?

I was once told never to begin a speech or a presentation with an apology. It takes away credibility from what you want to say. Similarly a disclaimer detracts from the validity of a message. A disclaimer is the lawyer's equivalent of an apology. Yet how many times will a lawyer begin advice by saying, "I may not have all the facts" or "based on the information available, which may or may not be reliable" or some other similar phrase that is intended in part at least to lay an escape route for the lawyer when real life turns up something unexpected.

We all know we do it and we all know why we do it. The effect on the reader, on the recipient of your advice, however, is exactly the same as the effect my disclaimer had on you.

Perception is reality

It is not just a slogan. Time and again relationships breakdown or become less valuable not because of a lack of legal expertise, not because of a lack of professionalism or care. Relationships breakdown and value is lost because people fail to appreciate what other people want, when they want it and how they want it. It is about understanding, empathy and communication. It is about emotional intelligence.

It is also a vast and largely untapped reservoir of long term, profitable and professionally rewarding work for those lawyers who see the opportunity and seize it.

Let us therefore at least start to address the clients' perceptions first and foremost; let us be less concerned with our own requirements and preferences and then let us see how even more successful and valued the profession may become as a result.

Chapter Six

The Harvard approach

In 1995 I read Roger Fisher's best-selling book on negotiation *'Getting to Yes'*. It was one of those moments that we all have when you realise that someone is articulating thoughts that you have held yourself. You are filled with a sense of gratitude that someone was able to make sense of your thoughts and present them in a way that reinforces your belief in them.

In that moment Roger Fisher became one of my heroes and I have wanted to meet him ever since. The more I have read about him and the more I have read about his work, the more of a hero he has become.

He teaches negotiation at Harvard Law School, where he is the Williston Professor of Law and Director of the world renowned Harvard Negotiation Project.

In the autumn of 2000 I travelled to Boston, Massachusetts to study negotiation skills in a workshop lead by Professor Fisher at the Harvard Law School and was not disappointed. In fact such was the impression made that I returned to study there again in the spring of 2001.

Professor Fisher's worldwide reputation is based on his work as an international negotiator, mediator and author. Someone who has been directly involved and influential in some of the most difficult and intractable problems the world's various political leaders have made for themselves in the last fifty years.

For many years he worked with successive government administrations in America as a special advisor to a number of Presidents. His credentials at the highest level are, I believe, unsurpassed by anyone in his field. In my opinion he is one of the great men of our time.

All this may be true (or I may just be a little star struck) but what, if anything, has any of this got to do with running legal services, in-house or in a law firm, in the United Kingdom, when (as far as I am aware) City law firms are not yet into overthrowing governments or holding diplomatic hostages in their basement archives?

It is actually fascinating and inspiring to hear directly from those involved how the Camp David Peace Accord was negotiated or how peace treaties were drafted between warring South American countries. However, the connection I made was a simple one. The issues that have to be addressed in these calamitous and literally world changing circumstances are always people issues.

In a nutshell, when the people involved can get on, the problems are easier to solve than when they do not.

International negotiation with all the pressure of expectant political forces and under the spotlight of the world's media is only different in scale but not substance from relationship management issues between lawyer and lawyer, and lawyer and client.

What I realised in 1995 when reading 'Getting to Yes' and had confirmed in 2000 in Boston is that relationship management is actually about negotiation and negotiation done well is about creating value to satisfy mutual interests.

The book is wholeheartedly recommended for its own sake, but I also recommend reading the book from a new perspective, one where the title is changed to read 'Getting more mutual value from the relationships with your clients'!

Over the next few pages I want to consider Roger Fisher's framework for negotiation, as he describes it in 'Getting to Yes', but in the context of relationship management and how, as a result, lawyers can add and create value for their clients, for their law firms or their legal departments and for themselves.

Professor Fisher describes seven different elements to successful negotiation. They are as follows:

- Identifying interests of all the parties involved

- Identifying options that may satisfy some or all of those interests

- Understanding your Best Alternative To A Negotiated

Agreement (otherwise referred to as your BATNA!)

- Establishing credibility both in yourself and in the options proposed as solutions

- Building relationships with all the parties involved

- Creating a communication strategy with all the parties involved

- Delivering on your commitments

Obviously in his book each of these elements is considered in turn in the context of negotiation. There are, however, many similarities for lawyers in the context of managing client relationships and I will now consider each of the seven elements in this context.

1. Identifying interests

In many ways this is probably the most significant of all the elements I will write about.

It is the most significant because, if this stage is understood properly, a better understanding of your own position and that of your client is inevitable. This fact almost of itself, without any other work, is enough to achieve a better understanding of needs and therefore allows for a better service to be given. As I will repeat often, from truly understanding interests comes long-term profitable relationships.

I sometimes notice with a wry smile the pronouncements made by law firms who clinch (good tabloid word) a place on a new client's panel. 'City & Co to act for ABC Inc' the headline will blaze. And, although this is newspaper-speak, it also creeps into the language of the law firm. Partners and associates talk about acting for corporations, multi-nationals, FTSE 250's and the like.

In fact they do nothing of the sort, law firms with corporate clients do not act for those businesses, they act for *people* in those businesses.

Law firms with corporate clients act for people who have bosses, subordinates and colleagues. Law firms with corporate clients act for people who have families, and homes and who want and need a life away from their offices. Law firms with corporate clients act for people who have ambitions, strengths and weaknesses and who from day to day may be feeling good, bad or indifferent about their work.

If you are consciously (or subconsciously) only acting for a brand, or a building, or an entry in the Financial Times listings, I can assure you that you will be providing a less effective service than if you were acting instead for the people associated by their contracts of employment with the said brand, building and entry in the Financial Times.

Before exploring this idea a little further, let me give you what is a hypothetical case study of the issues involved in identifying and understanding interests. The example is based on real events from the experiences of a number of different in-house lawyers whose shared experiences are brought together in this story.

In 1998 at the Annual General Meeting of a FTSE 250 company, the CEO made a statement heralding a multi-million pound investment in technology to transform the company's understanding of its customer databases. Once implemented service would improve, cross sales would skyrocket and fat bonuses for all directors would be the order of the day. (The CEO left out the last bit from the announcement.) It was a strategically significant announcement for the company and for the CEO who was staking his reputation on the hoped for benefits that would flow from the successful implementation of the project.

Just before the Annual General Meeting the board had met to discuss who would be the preferred supplier. Three major players had been in the tender process. The I.T. Director had previously worked for one of the companies and knew the sales team well. In truth they had made only the second best bid overall but were most competitive on price. The IT Director, however, made a strong case for them and the board were persuaded that there was considerable value in the working relationship the I.T. Director had already established.

The Finance Director, however, felt that the tender process was paramount and requested that the Minutes record his apprehension. He had also raised his concerns privately that the investment was too speculative and the returns promised were not actually promised.

This unease was also shared by the company Chairman, who did not think that an I.T. system (however amazing) was a substitute for having a good product to sell. The Chairman, however, felt that if the CEO wanted more rope to hang himself by then it would be churlish to gainsay the mood of the executive directors and, besides, it all just might work out in the end.

The fifth player in the drama was the Legal Director, who, shortly after the selection was confirmed instructed a large London firm to negotiate with the chosen supplier's legal team and to agree the various contractual arrangements that would need to be put in place.

Inevitably, all did not go well.

Budgets over-ran, timescales slipped, specifications changed. In the space of just eighteen months, eight million pounds had been spent but nothing more than unconnected tin boxes had been delivered.

The supplier blamed a constantly changing brief from the company and non-disclosure of pertinent matters at the tender stage.

The company blamed the incompetence of the supplier who had changed their team on the project three times in twelve months and who had failed to act on documents that had been disclosed. They had also claimed to have worked on similar deals for other companies but had in fact never worked on such a big project as this one.

It was a mess and the Legal Director went to the law firm that negotiated the terms of the deal for their advice.
But what is the law firm to do?

If the law firm simply takes its instructions from the Legal Director without an analysis or investigation of the competing and contradictory interests at stake, it has the potential to go horribly wrong. They may well prepare a claim based on the contractual documentation, argue the law and the facts from the company's perspective, never come close to being negligent and yet hugely disappoint their client.

If the law firm in our example acts just on the instruction from the Legal Director I am in fact certain that they will not impress, that they may actually antagonise their client and worst of all their hard work will be unrecognised, their billing will be challenged and their profitability damaged.

It is to be hoped that the Legal Director would help to reveal all the various interests at stake, but whether that is the case or not it should never be assumed. Let us look at all the various interests and how they potentially impact on the brief:

The Company, by which we mean the members and shareholders who want to see a return on their investment, both capital growth and income, and who want the company to be well regarded and well run.

The Board, who collectively take responsibility for the decision to invest with a particular supplier and who ultimately take responsibility for the successful management of the project.

The Company's customers, who would like the company to be successful on their behalf.

The Company's employees, who would also like the company to be successful on their behalf.

The CEO, who in less than six months must stand before the next Annual General Meeting and explain how his vision is in tatters (and therefore his reputation too) unless

70

there is a quick and decisive vindication through the courts or a capitulating settlement offered by the supplier, or best of all, the damn thing can be made to work.

The Chairman, who will now disassociate himself from the CEO and will want the best result possible for the shareholders and the City analysts. The share price is tumbling anyway and decisiveness is key. He is thinking whether there need to be high level resignations.

The I.T. Director, who is absolutely convinced that his personal relationship with the Supplier can pull the deal round. He just needs a few more weeks and progress will be seen. Faith is what is needed. Faith and a steady nerve. No major project like this one is without its setbacks. His view is that what has happened is par for the course.

The Finance Director, who never thought the project would deliver anyway, however successfully the project had been managed. He would simply like the eight million pounds returned and to start again.

The Legal Director, who believes the law firm to be truly excellent, but who has private reservations about instructing the same firm that negotiated the failing contracts.

The Company's I.T. project team, who will be key witnesses, all of whom have had really good one-to-one relations with the Supplier's people and who are both embarrassed at the position they are now in and fearful of attacks on them for incompetence.

The Supplier, who has invested resources and reputation in a strategically significant project and who is mooted as a possible takeover target by a U.S. conglomerate.

The Supplier's project team, who regularly reported their concerns at the unreasonable timeframe for the completion of the project to both Supplier and Company.

The Supplier's Board and senior management, of whom

we know little but whose attitudes and concerns we need to find out about if we are to have a chance of settling, particularly in the light of the takeover speculation.

The Supplier's insurer and the Company's insurer, who will both seek to claim material non-disclosure or will otherwise have found imaginative ways of not being on risk.

The law firm, which has a reputational stake in the conduct of the matter, which must make a certain economic return on the arrangements whatever the outcome and which would like to be seen as a forward thinking, client focused organisation.

In this one example are identified a total of fifteen separate interests.

We can also see that there are clearly interests within interests and it is almost certainly the case that there will be other interests here as well. We need to know what is motivating the senior players, what other deals and transactions are affected by the success or failure of the project, whether there are regulatory issues or corporate governance issues, and many more things besides, before we can really begin to adapt a legal service that will add value and be appreciated.

It is also the case that in reaching the understanding that there are just so many interests at stake, we can see how very sophisticated the law firm must be if it is to be seen (perception being reality) to have made a positive contribution.

This example also gives an insight into why law firms so often work incredibly hard on behalf of their clients and achieve a degree of success that is objectively more than acceptable or appropriate, but are still maligned by their clients for lacking focus and commerciality and for being too expensive.

Take, for example, the question of legal costs in the example.

The CEO would be prepared to spend whatever it takes to salvage the project or his reputation (preferably both). On the other hand the I.T. Director thinks that it is premature to have engaged lawyers at all and would not want to spend a single penny. If the Legal Director reports to the Finance Director other issues are in play. The phrase 'good money after bad' springs to mind for example.

The law firm will therefore get an entirely different response from the client to the question of their costs depending who within the client is responsible for the budget that will pay those costs.

This is just one small insight into understanding interests, but it is one that should be of seminal importance to all law firms. How many bills are discounted every day, often by significant amounts, to keep 'the client happy'? How often would that be necessary if the law firm had a strategy at the outset of their engagement for understanding the interests, not of the 'client, but of the person within the client responsible for paying the bills?

We have not even begun to consider how the fifteen different interests interact and influence the conduct of what is obviously a difficult dispute. Any strategy that is not based on trying to accommodate as many of the interests as possible will succeed more by luck than judgement. It is imperative therefore to identify and then understand as many of the interests as possible.

2. Identifying options

In terms of negotiation, identifying options is about being creative around possible solutions. In terms of managing relationships, identifying options is about the same thing. It is about finding the best way of dealing with given situations arising out of a need to reassure, persuade, and advise. It is about meeting the expectations of as many interests as possible and hence the need to have first identified those interests.

Professor Roger Fisher in 'Getting to Yes' uses a neat example to illustrate this point. He describes a scene where two little girls are arguing over who can have the last orange in the fruit bowl. Their mother hearing the commotion from another room comes into the kitchen to hear both girls proclaim their wish to have the last orange for themselves. The parent, takes the kitchen knife, slices the orange precisely in half and offers each child one half of the orange, both then burst into tears.

On the face of it there is nothing much wrong with the mother's strategy. It is fair and easy to implement. It has the advantage of speed and would stand independent scrutiny from a third party arbiter such as the girls' father!

However the mother did not explore the interests of the children before she settled upon her chosen solution. Had she done so she would have been told that one daughter wanted the orange to eat because she was hungry and the second daughter wanted to make a cake and needed the orange peel.

On hearing this information a new and wholly different solution becomes obvious, one that satisfies both sets of interests completely.

It is clear to me that better solutions will be found when, and only when, all interests are identified and, in so far as they can be, those interests are addressed by the solutions proposed.

There is another significant advantage to adopting this approach. It gives the lawyer permission to be creative in the solutions he or she finds. Another analogy and a real life example demonstrate this approach.

The analogy, which I borrow from Professor Lawrence Susskind at the Massachusetts Institute of Technology, goes like this. Two lawyers are in a room negotiating over the division of a number of gold coins. There are precisely one hundred gold coins in the bowl. The mediator, who is supervising the negotiation, leaves the room requesting that the lawyers negotiate a fair allocation of gold coins between them.

An hour later the mediator returns. She sees that each lawyer has in front of him twenty-five gold coins with fifty gold coins left in the bowl. In slightly surprised tones the mediator asks the lawyers to explain the division.

Lawyer #1 says that his client's instructions were to get no less than twenty-five gold coins. He, having achieved that number, felt that his work was done.

Lawyer #2 says that his client's instructions were to get no less than the number given to the client of lawyer #1.

The lawyers believed their clients would be happy with the result. I suspect the clients may not see it that way.

Now in the real world, no one reading this analogy will think 'actually that is a good result'. You will not think it is a good result because you can clearly see that there are fifty more gold coins begging to be lifted out of the bowl to add more value to the deal for the clients.

But what if you did not know there were one hundred gold coins? What if you had no idea if there were fifty gold coins or five hundred gold coins? Then, many more of you would think the deal that was reached was a reasonable one, if not a spectacular one.

The point, of course, is that in most negotiations, in most deals, in most relationships we do not know how much value there is to be had. We may have a good idea, but, until we have explored interests, we have no licence to explore options. In the Susskind analogy had the lawyers considered what their clients' interests were instead of accepting the instructions they received, it is entirely likely (we can hope anyway) that the remaining fifty gold coins would have been divided up as well.

In the real world, where we do not necessarily know how much value we may find, add or create, we should also take time to explore whether there are other options, other approaches that might reveal hidden value.

The real world example involves a large London firm advising a FTSE 250 company through a takeover. From the law firm's point of view there was nothing terribly difficult or unusual about the deal. They have a track record and an acknowledged expertise in the area. From the client's perspective, by which we mean the board (its directors individually), the shareholders and employees (etc), it was the single biggest deal in their lives. It was a deal that for them had the potential to transform their world of work for the better or to end in misery.

This was a wonderful opportunity for the law firm, with all its experience and reputation, to put a nervous client at its ease and develop really significant opportunities for value for years to come.

The law firm throughout the transaction, however, treated the client like a novice spectator at an avant-garde operatic performance. The client was initially very eager to please and to understand what the hell was going on, but the law firm kept making the equivalent of an admonishing 'tut-tut' sound every time the client clapped in the wrong place or rustled a sweet wrapper during a quiet part of the performance.

By the end of the transaction the law firm was congratulating itself on another big bill, the client was so disengaged that it was hard to imagine there had been any relationship at all.

After this traumatic event for the client, was the law firm asked to help with all the related pensions advice, employment advice, contracts negotiations, litigation, intellectual property matters, premises issues and the like?

No, they were not.

The law firm had just one bill for their six months work, but they could have had a monthly bill for years to come. All that was needed was for the law firm to treat the client as if the deal was as important to them as it was to the client; to sit down with the client and show that it cared, to explore the concerns and anxieties of the client and to look for the small details that would reassure and comfort the client.

Had the law firm developed one single idea that they then presented to the client as a unique piece of work for a unique client, the relationship would have blossomed. Instead it died.

Every relationship, every deal has potential beyond the obvious. Lawyers have a special opportunity to unlock hidden value because they have privileged access and insights into the their clients' minds.

Any lawyer who spends the time to find value will not only have a more appreciative client, but they will also have a more profitable client.

3. Best Alternative To a Negotiated Agreement (BATNA)

In any negotiation situation 'win or bust' strategies are high risk and not generally to be recommended. Even so people talk all the time about their 'bottom line' and this appears to be the point at which the deal will collapse because it holds insufficient value. If that is what they actually mean, then it is effectively a win or bust strategy.

Perhaps what they mean, however, is to describe the point at which their best alternative to a negotiated agreement kicks in. Their BATNA in other words.

Roger Fisher in 'Getting to Yes' describes the importance of developing a BATNA. The more attractive it becomes, the more value it holds, then the easier it becomes to negotiate for the deal you actually want. In the Boston workshop he described how he advised a young lawyer looking for a move to one of the Chicago law firms.

The lawyer had had three interviews with three different firms and had just received a job offer from one of them but at a salary he could barely afford to accept. He desperately wanted the job but he did not know how to even begin the conversation that would have him say that despite wanting the job he needed more money. He felt his negotiating position was far too weak.

Fisher told him to look for an alternative job in his second city of choice. This happened to be St Louis. He told him to give it his best shot but when it came to talking about salary to stand firm and ask for what he felt was a fair package for the job.

Within a couple of weeks he had secured an interview and was then offered a great job with the salary he wanted. It was in his second choice city but it was fine in every other respect.

Fisher then told him to go back to the Chicago firm that had been his first choice to request that they at least match the offer he had in his pocket. If they truly wanted him, they would pay;

if they refused to pay, he had a super alternative to fall back on.

The Chicago firm improved their offer and the lawyer got the job, the city and the salary he wanted. It is a classic example of how to make a seemingly weak position stronger by building a BATNA.

The point to draw out from an understanding of this negotiation technique is that it can and should be applied to the way in which we manage relationships.

Whether you are an in-house lawyer or work for a law firm you will have a complex number of relationships to manage each and every day. These will include:

- Your boss (and possibly his or her boss too)

- Your team including all your support staff

- Colleagues in other legal teams

- Colleagues in H.R., I.T., Training, Marketing and other support functions

- Your client contacts, their staff and their stakeholders.

Each relationship has a character of its own. Some will be business-like, some will be fun, some will be difficult and sometimes these characteristics will change from day to day. Each relationship impacts on your ability to deliver an outstanding, value-adding service to your client. It is therefore imperative, it seems to me, that we all avoid 'win or bust' strategies with these relationships. They each need to be nurtured and developed, their interests understood and options developed to help the relationships work to your advantage when you need them to.

But you also need to understand the consequences of those relationships not working: what the impact will be on the task in hand, on the client relationship, on the reputation of the team and you. If the relationship, or any one relationship, does not work, what is the alternative and how can that alternative be made to work as effectively as possible?

What does this mean in practical terms?

When working for a building society I did a lot of work in their marketing department approving their advertising copy. It was interesting and fun and obviously very important too. The work was characterised by short bursts of frenetic activity with impossibly short deadlines. Advertising agencies only ever seem to produce their material with seconds to spare. I assume this is something to do with the artistic temperament, but it is a pain in the backside from a compliance point of view!

Over a period of time I built up excellent relationships within the marketing team. We got on well and the work was always managed with good humour and in a professional and helpful way.

I was ill and off work for five weeks. The relationships I had built up over a couple of years then broke down in an instant because while there was sympathy all round for everyone's plight, there was no mechanism in place to service the sign-off needs of the marketing department.

It is possible (and quite right) to argue that this was a simple risk management issue and that a good management process would have ensured that there was someone in the team who could cover or an external law firm primed to step in.

It is also possible, and preferable, to view this situation as my failure to develop a BATNA.

I was on a 'win or bust' strategy with my client with a very weak BATNA. Had I realised this at the time then I could have spent time developing the best alternative to the service some thought about what the client might prefer in my absence (colleague or law firm) and developed the new relationships to a point where everyone would feel reassured that the service I was providing would continue in my absence.

Some lawyers will recoil slightly at the mention of 'risk management'. Their facial expressions change and they put on the air of people who have been told that this is an important phrase, but have little idea what it actually means in practice.

It might just be that lawyers who are uncomfortable with notions of risk management in their practice areas will be more comfortable with and understanding of what their BATNA means to them and their clients.

It is another example of building and managing relationships to add value that in turn is more likely than not to result in a better service, a more appreciative client and, therefore, a more profitable client.

4. Establishing credibility

In Professor Fisher's book the fourth element in the seven stages of a successful negotiation is about establishing objective criteria to judge the credibility of an offer. In other words do not just accept at face value the claim of the other side that they are "only prepared to pay £500, take it or leave it", but ask "why £500?"

Find out if the offer is based on objective and verifiable criteria that will allow you to judge whether the offer is reasonable or not.

What is the relevance of establishing credibility when managing relationships?

Establishing credibility is essential to stabilising a new relationship and adding value to an existing relationship. There are two areas to cover:

- The credibility of the profession as a whole.

- How lawyers may individually gain credibility in their work.

When my daughter was five years old she asked me what I did for a job. I told her I was a lawyer and (seeing the bemused look on her face) I told her that lawyers were people who helped other people with their problems.

She said, "I see, like a nurse or the lollypop lady at school"

I told her that it was not quite like being a nurse or a lollypop lady and tried to explain that lawyers help people who have been naughty and also help people who have had naughty things done to them. Then, struggling with trying to describe what I had done for the last twenty odd years, went on to say that lawyers also help people when they want to change houses (though they did not usually move furniture) and to help run their businesses.

At that point I stopped as I had confused the poor girl enough, but in a slightly surreal moment I imagined that her adult response to what I had said might have been to say,

"Well that is all very well, but I do not see why any of those things should need a lawyer to do them and anyway, what will you do when a public defender system is introduced, the banks do all the conveyancing and the accountancy firms run all the businesses?"

You have to think that this is a fair point. Why should lawyers feel that certain work is automatically their right? And, as if to prove the point, nearly everyone can see that there is increased competition; that there has been an erosion of certain markets and, worst of all, a significant loss of reputation. This in part has been encouraged by a generally superficial and hostile tabloid press, so that very many people believe that lawyers are either fat cats or incompetent, or both.

While being prepared to argue forcefully that lawyers are hardworking, creative and committed to their clients, there clearly is a perception problem and it is likely that the perception is significantly damaging the ability of all lawyers to defend existing markets and, even more importantly, to enter new ones.

Many of these perception issues can be traced back to the early and mid-1980s when the profession seemed to turn its back on what marketing types would call its core values and, at the same time, decided to play in the Thatcherite playground called the 'marketplace'.

There are two problems with this:

- First; 'lawyer' is a damn good brand and the core values that underpin the brand (like 'honour', 'trust', 'care', 'attention to detail', 'expertise' and 'independence of mind') should be as obvious to people as the brand values are to those people who buy Coca Cola, Dyson vacuum cleaners or Virgin air tickets. Neglecting to enhance, promote and live up to the brand values was and is stupid.

- Second; while competing in the marketplace is a necessity, it requires a mastery of cost control, of investment strategy, of sales techniques and of information technology, and also a concept of a product that can be packaged and repackaged to meet sectoral interests when markets become complex and diversify. I doubt that even today law firms can claim to be able to do this to a consistently high standard.

The result has been that great swathes of work have been lost to accountancy firms and to other business people who can spot a market, design a process, package a product and manage a margin.

There is though a way back.

Business issues will be covered in much more detail later in the book. For now, it can be said that lawyers are very well equipped to be business people, but they really must get a grip on how to run their own businesses. Even those very clever magic circle firms who earn millions in invisible imports have to understand that you cannot going on hiking the cost of your product to pay staff and partners huge salaries and not find that your customers are less than impressed.

However successful things may appear to be today, it only takes one prick to burst a bubble and I do not believe that the City is free of pricks.

If law firms really do not want to spend time developing and innovating business models, then they must employ business professionals who can do it for them.

Most importantly, lawyers must also restore and promote their brand and in particular they must capture the high ground of their core values. This for me is summed up by a single word, 'trust'.

Trust is like the air we breathe. You cannot touch it or see it, but let it go and the body will surely die.

I believe that self-regulation is a talisman for the profession in this regard. The message it sends is 'trusted to regulate itself'. It is the most exclusive and hard won of kite marks and the profession must be seen to invest even more in what is the biggest symbol of high ethical standards, of excellence in conduct and business probity. Ethical (and always commercial) conduct should have the highest profile in all training in law colleges and in in-house programmes and it should be used as part of a concerted and bold brand building exercise.

It is, as we know, a uniquely competitive world, but self-regulation is a unique selling point; it is our U.S.P.

The credibility that comes from trust, from being seen to uphold the highest possible standards, is the entry ticket to the inner sanctums of the business world. It is where advice can add the highest possible value and where long-term relationships are forged.

To stand outside and only be able to knock on the door with every other consultant, adviser and half qualified chancer is to diminish the brand and our value to businesses and the wider community to such an extent as to be almost criminal.

Credibility is competitive advantage; competitive advantage is success.

So how do legal teams, law firms and individual lawyers get credibility with their clients?

The answer is in building and managing relationships with them, not in a formulaic 'by numbers' manner but with genuine empathy and a human touch. This brings us to the fifth element in the Fisher negotiation model.

5. Building relationships

Building and managing relationships is about spatial awareness.

Most lawyers (actually most people) are selfish creatures of habit. In work, as in life, we are motivated predominantly by our own hopes, fears and what we can achieve for ourselves. This is not a criticism, merely an observation. We all tend to walk around in a self-built bubble that allows us to see what we want to see and which filters the rest. It is called our comfort zone.

In our comfort zone the world behaves in a predictable way. On the whole it treats us well and, while we may complain, sometimes a lot, about our lot, its familiarity helps to signpost our lives. A comfort zone is like having our very own satellite navigation system prompting the direction of our lives.

Many of us would prefer to have a clear route to somewhere, even when that somewhere is not very special, than to have no road map at all in a world full of wonderful opportunity.

As lawyers we know what we are good at, we know the way we like to work with clients and colleagues and we know what we enjoy. When looking for friendship we tend to be attracted to people who share at least some of our perceptions of the world, but when looking for clients it would be an amazing coincidence if they all shared our likes and dislikes. So we will clearly not always get clients that make us feel comfortable.

The point is that while we can all retreat to our comfort zones from time to time, building and managing successful relationships with clients is about working in their comfort zones, not ours.

In Chapter Five I set out the 'perception test' where the interplay between client and lawyer clearly shows that often the actual differences between them are not great but the perception gaps are sometimes massive.

A few years ago I took a test about discrimination awareness. One example in a quick-fire series of questions was about a heart surgeon operating on a child. The facts were presented in such a way that you knew there was a family relationship between the heart surgeon and child. The question required a simple statement of the nature of the relationship. The answer, as soon as it was revealed, was completely obvious but I, and most other people who took the test with me, got it wrong.

The surgeon was the child's mother.

Subconsciously I had discounted the possibility of the heart surgeon being a woman. I viewed the question from the safety of my comfort zone, where I see what I want to see and I discount the rest. It is so easy to retreat into our comfort zone, but it is like putting on a blindfold. It stops us seeing.

The first lesson of building and managing relationships is to be aware of one's own comfort zone, to accept its limitations but then to deal with it. Then you are equipped to at least begin to see the comfort zones that others occupy.

That's what I mean by spatial awareness.

Let me give you an example.

In one recent consultancy project I was working with a small team of marketing lawyers. An issue had arisen whereby the marketing professionals were starting to feel that the lawyers had become too cautious in their advice. Examples of competitors' advertisements were routinely sent to the legal team with somewhat caustic remarks about 'How come they can get away with it?' A suggestion had also been made by a senior manager that perhaps the marketing team should self-certify advertising copy.

When I discussed the problem with the lawyers, their reaction was very consistent; the marketing team want the impossible. They want complicated matters signed-off in an instant, they want to ride roughshod over regulations and the legal team is under-resourced in any event.

In my experience marketing people have always wanted the impossible. They have never had a regard for others and they would much prefer to be able to say that their product was the best, the cheapest and the whizziest there had ever been. By the way, they would also like to say that everyone else's product was rubbish!

It is also my experience that every legal team there has ever been has wanted more resources.

I did not hear anything therefore that made me think that I had heard the real reason for this relationship failing in such a serious way.

Two years previously the marketing team and the lawyers had shared the same floor of the same building. The relationship then was said to have been excellent. It was characterised by lots of involvement in the ideas stage of planning a marketing campaign. There was social interaction with people lunching together and meeting at coffee machines to pass the time of day and the perception was that sign-off by the lawyers happened more quickly.

Then, because the company was growing so fast, the lawyers were moved out to another building a few hundred yards away. The lawyers stayed at their desks, the interaction slowly diminished and the relationships cooled. Interestingly the sign-off procedures showed that turnaround times had actually improved since the move!

It would be very superficial to draw a conclusion that living with the client will help to build relationships.

The lawyers had not actually behaved any differently when they were co-located with the their client. They had not realised that they were inadvertently pressing the right buttons with the marketing team, so that when the lawyers left, their behaviour did not change to compensate for the fact they were no longer close by. They believed they were carrying on as before and could not understand why the relationship began to deteriorate.

As the relationship slowly deteriorated, the lawyers were powerless (they felt) to do anything about it. What was happening was being done to them because they were acting in the same way as they had always acted. The lawyers retreated into a comfort zone of supporting each other, of viewing missives from the marketing team as if they were hostile incursions and of relying on a service standard agreement that dictated the appropriate sign-off procedure.

The marketing team thought the lawyers had become aloof and unhelpful.

What had actually happened was that before the move the legal team was working in the marketing team's comfort zone. The lawyers were known faces, available and involved. Without thinking the lawyers were building and managing relationships in a way that the marketing team wanted. When they left the physical confines of the building the lawyers also left their client's comfort zone and even though, ironically, by one measure the service had improved, the perception all round was that the relationship had fallen part.

The solution, however, was very straightforward. In order to recover the position the lawyers had simply to consciously and visibly reoccupy the marketing team's comfort zone (and also step out of their own comfort zone). They had to become visible again. They had to be seen and show themselves to be the friendly, concerned, non-aloof individuals they were before, except that this time they would have to do it from a different building.

Here is another example to illustrate the point. One of the more senior partners of a national law firm was telling me how delighted he was to have secured a new client following a beauty parade in which his firm had been involved.

He explained, however, how that throughout the presentation he had felt that the client was not properly engaged in the process. It all felt a little distant and he was sure they had not done very well. After the presentation (which had been the last of three that day) the client thanked the senior partner for an excellent presentation but the words sounded rehearsed and not terribly genuine.

On the way home from his presentation, the partner told me that he thought that things had not gone too well and this thought began to eat away at him. He decided to phone the client from his car.

"I just thought I would call," he told a slightly surprised head of legal. "Only I wondered if everything was okay; I had the feeling that things didn't quite gel today for you. Was it a bad day back in the office?"

The head of legal opened up almost immediately. There had been a significant mistake made in the timing of a product launch and the whole thing was a bit of a mess. One hour later, the partner had organised a team from his firm to be at the offices of the client the next morning.

I asked him why he made the call when most would have gone home and not thought about the presentation again until they heard the result from the client. He told me that he thought he had lost the presentation, that the client was not engaging with him and that, if he was right, there might just have been a reason for it and finding out if there was a reason was worth the call.

The client, on the other hand realised that here was someone who had stepped away from his own comfort zone and had sensed his discomfort. The client knew straightaway that anyone capable of sensing the world he lived in would be the lawyer to hire.

There is not anything in this story that is revelatory. There is nothing terribly innovative or cutting edge. All that has happened is that one human being has reacted in a human way to another human being's discomfort. You may not find this approach in a service level agreement or in a management manual, but it works.

(A suitable point, perhaps, to note that if your firm has invested a small fortune in an imposing marbled entrance hallway and reception area, you might pause to think why you are trying to be 'imposing' and to reflect therefore on the messages you are actually sending to the human representatives of your corporate clients.)

Finally, one more example in this section but this one perhaps noting a more typical reaction.

I was recently working with another law firm and debriefing a partner who had been experiencing some problems establishing a relationship with a key client of the firm. She had just called the client as part of a regular pattern of courtesy calls and I asked her how the call had gone.

She told me that the client had said that it was a bad time to call because he had a bit of a crisis on just now and she therefore offered to call him back at a more convenient moment. He said he would get back to her.

On the face of it, she did not do anything wrong but it would be hard to say the relationship had improved as a result of her call and perhaps it just got a little worse.

Here was a heaven sent opportunity to offer some real help, to show the firm cared about the relationship in a 'we're in it together' way that would secure loyalty and demonstrate commitment that cannot always be bought at any price.

Building relationships is so important. Clients are lost every day not through error or negligence (we have already seen how the right answer is not always what the client needs anyway) but through our failure to see, to listen and to act in ways that show the client that we are aware of them.

This goes back to another point made earlier on. We do not act for corporations, we act for people.

Although this section has been a little 'touchy-feely', it ends on a practical note.

Far too many relationships between law firm and company are established between just two individuals, the lawyer in the law firm and the in-house lawyer or business manager for the company. This is a very fragile arrangement and, while the relationship may be very strong, it is also vulnerable.

What happens, for example, when the lawyer moves on, or the business manager is promoted? What happens if a mistake is made? What happens if the lawyer is tied up elsewhere?

The strength of a relationship should not be measured by how just two points of contact get on (important though that obviously is); the strength of a relationship is in having many points of contact, in having a multi-layered approach.

The more points of contact and the more unplanned those contacts points can be, the better the relationship will be, both in terms of the longevity of the relationship and its profitability. It is about being seen to be part of the client team, in for the long haul, and helpful at any level.

To many this will sound odd. Many firms seem to thrive on the basis of key clients and lead partners who jealously guard any access to their precious cash cows. Just from a risk management point of view, it cannot be a good idea to have so much invested in the hands of one person and in his or her ability to manage a complex relationship that might break down at any time for any number of unpredictable reasons.

Such an approach has more to do with the insecurity of certain partners than the long-term profitability and success of a relationship between law firm and client.

An ideal model for managing such relationships is found later in this book.

6. Creating a communication strategy

This is the sixth element of the Fisher negotiation model. Communication problems are a cliché; everyone has them to a greater or lesser extent. Ask anyone what is wrong with a relationship (any relationship) and sooner or later they will say 'communication'.

So all you have to do, therefore, is do a little more communication and all will be well with the world. Well, not quite.

By now we are seeing that certain themes in relationship management repeat themselves, inter-react and interconnect.

One of these themes is that 'perception is reality', which has become something of a personal mantra. It does, however, refocus my mind in any given situation so that I am always trying to think from the perspective of the person/people I am dealing with as well as my own perspective of the world.

We have also seen that unless we identify and deal with the interests that others have we will not engage their attention except in a very superficial way. In order to be able to see other people's interests we know that we must step outside of our own comfort zones to be able to see the world through their eyes.

If you are able to do all this, then you have the opportunity to build and manage successful, long term and profitable relationships. The key to turning this potential into reality is to ensure that clients can see, hear and sense that you are working on their behalf and in their interests.

On one occasion one of my in-house team wanted to have a word with me about how he had felt taken for granted by a particular business team. The week previously he had given up a day's annual leave and had worked past midnight to complete a contract negotiation so that a new computer system would be ordered in time to qualify for a significant price discount.

He sent the completed contract to the relevant executive for her to sign. She sent it back duly signed, but with no note of thanks or any recognition at all of his efforts.

I asked him whether he had explained to anyone what he would be personally required to do on behalf of the business team or whether he had subsequently explained to anyone what he had actually now achieved on their behalf?

Inevitably he said he had been too busy and he assumed people would realise the amount of work involved.

That was not a good enough reply.

If clients do not know what work you are doing on their behalf how on earth do you expect them to value your work? If your clients cannot value your contribution why should you expect them to feel good about paying for it?

A simple email, or better still a phone call, would have allowed clients a view on the lawyer's world. Let the client see the complexity, the ingenuity and the sheer hard work and they are bound to appreciate more your efforts on their behalf.

If you force spectators to stay outside the football stadium, they are unlikely to want to pay the admission charge, however good the game is.

Time and again lawyers seem to complain that their clients have little or no idea how difficult something is, how they have to weigh up any number of issues with competing priorities and how changing circumstances can impact on their deliberations. It is clear that lawyers are prepared to work tirelessly for their clients, but if the same lawyers do not invest a little time in telling their clients about the work they are doing, the clients will not fill in the gaps for themselves.

Alongside *'perception is reality'*, another little saying of mine to help focus attention on issues such as this one, is *'hope is not a strategy'*.

I can remember reminding my teams regularly of this point whenever they started a sentence, "But I assumed that…"

It is not that it is always wrong to make assumptions, but too often the assumptions we make are based on *our* own perception of a problem, issue or project and not the perceptions of the other people involved with us.

To assume anything is to gamble with expectation and hope. Hoping something may be right is nowhere near as effective as setting out with a strategy to ensure that something is right.

Lawyers, both in law firms and in in-house teams, were asked how they communicate with their clients. Like everyone else in business they communicate by:

- Letter, email, meetings and telephone calls,

- Seminars and training events,

- Circulars and brochures, and

- Hospitality events.

It is a standard set of responses with absolutely no surprises.

It can be deduced from this that all lawyers, by and large, are communicating with their clients in the same way and from the quality of some brochures and events it is clear that a great deal of money is invested in communication.

Yet we know that not all lawyers communicate as well as each other, or (presumably) as well as they all would like.

This was amply demonstrated by the fact that when the same lawyers were asked how they gauged the success of their communications, most shrugged their shoulders and said that they 'hoped' they communicated with their clients in the way their clients wanted.

Hope, however, as we now know is not a strategy and communication is far too important an element of any relationship to leave to the whim of chance.

The essential point is it is not how a message is *given* that is important (however glossy the brochure may be); it is how the message is *received* that makes the difference and this is where value in relationships may be created.

To an extent most of us do understand this point already, but it is more an intuitive response to certain situations rather than a thought-through working practice or strategy.

We would not explain a complicated point about a technical issue to a lay person in the same way as we would when talking to a colleague. I am not sure however that we have a very much more sophisticated answer than this to the question of how we evaluate the best ways of allowing clients, colleagues and contacts to receive our messages.

Too often we explain the results of poor communication by claiming that someone else is being 'difficult', and the results of good communication by saying that people just 'clicked'. Neither response to the issue of what makes communication work (or not work) is acceptable.

We need to understand what makes communication work and what individuals want from us when we set out to communicate with them.

In addition to (perhaps instead of) all the time and money that is already spent on the process of creating the messages we want to give (through our brochures, reports and other corporate communications), we should also spend a modest fraction of that time and money on the process of understanding how easily and effectively those messages are received. Then we would be in a far better position to exploit value-adding opportunities than we are today.

This does not just apply to marketing literature; it applies to every letter, every phone call and every email. Every communication, however seemingly unimportant, is loaded with opportunity to make a positive or negative contribution to the underlying relationship. Communication is all pervading and all-important.

The 'Identifying interests' section above described the example of the dispute between a company and their technology supplier. In describing the complex interplay between the various directors and potential witnesses it was obvious that the communication issues arising as a result of the dispute were going to be immensely complicated.

These issues have to be understood and handled in the context of that dispute as in every other matter, not in the context of what suits the lawyers. Far too often lawyers communicate in ways to suit themselves rather in ways to suit the client and those individuals working within the client.

The irony is, of course, that it is almost certainly to the lawyer's advantage (both in terms of time and profitability) to carefully select the ways and means of communicating with clients rather than to assume that the way the lawyer usually works will always be best. In doing so, the client is likely, at the very least, to be more engaged and have more understanding of the issues. That can only be a good thing.

Back with our dispute with the I.T. supplier, what might be the communication strategy?

If, for example, the Finance Director of the client company held the purse strings in the case, then he should be one of the players identified and targeted by the law firm to be their champion at the board table regarding the merits of going to court.

How might they seek to persuade him that going to court is a viable option?

(Remember this is not just about the merits of the arguments for or against; it is also about how the arguments are presented.)

In the circumstances, the law firm might approach the communication issues by:

• Preparing a report concentrating mainly on a persuasive economic argument justifying the proposed course of action and weighing up the financial risks and benefits.

• Dealing very specifically with their own costs and giving some empirical indicator of the chances of success.

• Considering whether the F.D. would prefer the report to be in writing (as opposed to being given orally in a meeting) and whether it should be prepared well in advance of the board meeting with an opportunity offered to deal with any supplementary points before the board meeting, again in writing.

As a very brief summary of what might be involved, this may or may not describe the correct approach for this particular Finance Director, but it is an approach to communication based on the perceived needs of the Finance Director and not the house style of the law firm.

If on the other hand the Chief Executive was the prime mover at the board table, a potentially different approach may be called for:

• Obviously an economic case must be made. (The F.D. must still be persuaded after all.)

• Given the background a more emotional, principled case might also be put. This would perhaps lead the law firm to offer, in addition to their written report, to attend the board meeting in person to explain the options to the directors and to be seen to support the Chief Executive.

It is not suggested that these alternatives are the right options, but we have to be constantly thinking of the alternative communication strategies that might work in each of our cases and for the individuals involved in them. Above all we must avoid imposing our own communication preferences on our clients without thinking how they will be perceived by them.

Communication done well requires a strategy, and hope, in this area, is definitely not a strategy.

7. Delivering on commitments

Delivering on commitments, as a factor in managing relationship, sounds so obvious as almost to go without saying. Yet it is so important that at least a few paragraphs are justified. It is also the last of the seven elements of the Professor Fisher negotiation model.

Fisher's great achievement is in setting out his vision of what he calls 'principled negotiation' is to challenge every assumption we ever had that negotiation was all about positional bargaining and the notion that the perceived strongest proponent will always win.

The framework he sets out demonstrates that any negotiation can improve any given position if the seven stages he describes are followed, and this is regardless of how weak we consider our starting position to be, even more so when the relationship that is established as a result of the negotiation is envisaged to be for the long term (as opposed to a one-off transitory arrangement). In these situations, where long term relations are important for all involved, the negotiation is more about establishing a process by which the parties can relate to each other. This process, as a result, is therefore almost more important that the actual outputs of that negotiation.

By way of example the 'Good Friday' agreement that has governed the peace process in Northern Ireland in recent times has been criticised for any number of perceived weaknesses by all sides. It has, however, established a process for the parties involved to come together. While the process stays in place (it does not always have to flourish), the actual tangible improvements all sides say they want and require are at least potentially achievable, if not achieved.

Similarly, the breakdown in the Middle East peace process in 2000-2001 saw a dramatic escalation in hostilities between warring factions - not because the issues are any more intractable than they ever were, but because the process has collapsed within which these sworn enemies might have had any sort of non-aggressive interface with each other.

In obviously more modest ways, personal relationships between lawyers and business clients need to operate within a framework that allows people to understand interests, generate solutions, establish credibility, build relationships and communicate with each other.

Without the framework, relationships are blown in the winds of fate; sometimes the winds are kindly, at other times they are not.

What is abundantly clear is that however good the relationships might be, what is needed to justify a fee or salary (for law firm or in-house team) is a job well done.

That means delivering on commitments.

Nothing builds trust more quickly and more firmly that achieving results. This therefore requires very careful management and much more care than the majority of lawyers seem to understand. Like having a communication strategy, it is also too important to leave to chance.

Three areas to consider:

- Giving the right message about results
- Finding further opportunities to add value, and
- Linking results to performance.

Giving the right message about results

How often is the result lost in the whirl of activity at the end of a matter? How often do lawyers say, "Hardly does one matter finish than the next one begins"? How often do we stop to think what the client is thinking at the point of completion or judgement?

It is that last point that is so important. One senior in-house lawyer told me how she had been working on a big corporate deal, one that was modest by City standards but the biggest event in her company's history.

There had been the usual long hours, lots of travel, meetings at short notice and plenty of stress. On the day of completion she was at the offices of the lawyers handling the transaction, together with her Finance Director (who had been involved from the start with her) and the Chief Executive. He had flown in from Florida that morning, shortening his family holiday by a few days to be available for any last minute hassles.

At the appointed hour the courier arrived with the relevant suite of signed documents, which were then duly countersigned. There was some perfunctory hand shaking and a glass of wine was summoned up from the caterers, but within 15 minutes the in-house lawyer and her two executive directors were left on their own in their windowless meeting room and told that they could leave whenever it was convenient for them; reception would order cabs for them.

Many people reading this account will not consider that anything untoward has happened, but now consider the conversation that took place between the three people left in the meeting room.

The CEO said with irritation bordering on anger, "Have I flown all the way back from the States just for that?"

The Finance Director said to the in-house lawyer, "Did you say this would cost us about two hundred thousand pounds? There was more to buying my house than what's happened here! I have not seen anything today to justify that sort of money"

And the in-house lawyer said to them both, "They really have done a good job for us, but perhaps we are not such an important client that they want to make a fuss of us".

If the senior partner of the law firm responsible for the transaction had heard this he might not have believed his ears, because he was the same senior partner who had:

- Supervised the weeks of effort that went into the deal.

- Required a team of four lawyers to work through the last seventy-two hours virtually without a break and

- Who had only just persuaded the finance department to knock a few thousand off the bill so that it would come in at just under two hundred thousand pounds.

But, the client genuinely could not see that commitments had been delivered, only that a few bundles of documents had been exchanged between law firms.

And because the law firm treated the transaction as nothing out of the ordinary, the client was left with no way of understanding its true value.

One is tempted to note that even God did not leave the human race on its own to work out whether it had got a good deal out of Creation. He at least found a few people to write a manual for him to explain what he had done. Presumably this was so that the full complexity of the deal was set out in detail and the credit was given where the credit was due!

What should the law firm have done?

The law firm should have made the CEO feel like visiting royalty. They should have realised that if the Big Cheese was flying back from holiday he would be in need of some stroking and made to feel that his contribution, however modest, was crucial to the success of the deal.

The law firm should also have taken the Finance Director to one side and explained how the economics of the deal had been achieved and how well they had actually managed their own margin so that they were now in a position to pass on a significant discount (which had been agreed that very day despite everything else that was going on).

The law firm should also have seen that their biggest ally for this deal and future deals was the in-house lawyer. They should have taken her behind the scenes and shown her the engine room, made her feel part of the inner sanctum and a player in their team. They should have made her feel special.

What would all this have cost?

Hardly anything, just a little thought and little more time, and a lot less than a disgruntled client with a CEO and a Finance Director who may never want to use the firm again.

Finding further opportunities to add value

The very best time to drive home positive messages about law firms and lawyers is at the completion of a transaction or conclusion of a trial etc. Whether things are seen to have gone well or badly, value can be created for all involved by taking some time to understand what went well and what should have been done better.

Three things should happen as a result:

- First; the lawyers can explain what they have done and why it was done in ways that (hopefully) answer any misgivings or misconceptions the client may have. If those misconceptions and misgivings are not addressed by the explanations the lawyers give, the lawyers at least have the client's undivided attention and can explore the ways to redress any grievances. It is so important not to let the client go without taking this opportunity to put things right.

- Second; direct feedback from the client in respect of a real transaction (not a training exercise) can and should allow for refinements to be made to the service offered by the law firm. No process has ever been invented that could not be improved. This echoes one of the points made at the beginning of the book about competitive advantage. It is the small changes that should be made to constantly improve a service that allow value to flow from law firm to client and vice versa.

• Third; it is a wonderful selling opportunity. The client has been persuaded to use the lawyer (the hardest part of all) and the lawyer has met (hopefully exceeded) the client's expectations. So, are you going to leave them alone in an airless box masquerading as a meeting room with a limp sandwich and warm orange juice? Or are you going to seize the best chance you will ever get with that particular client to make them realise that yours is the best law firm they could ever use?

The same points can made for in-house lawyers working with their business contacts.

Selling a service is not easy, selling value is even harder, but when you have just done something amazing you can do both so much more easily because you have something tangible to relate to.

During the course of a deal or trial, lawyers and clients go through what might be weeks or even months of close contact. As lawyers, what might you learn about your clients as a result?

If you have even half an eye open you will see what the pressing issues of the day might be; you will see where the balance of power may lie, who holds the purse strings and what attitudes there are towards using outside professional help. You will form a judgement on whether the business is well run or otherwise; you may also see where your law firm could provide additional support.

As the matter you are instructed on progresses, continue to gather all the intelligence you will ever need to be persuasive about offering more help in more areas.

It is the best opportunity most law firms ever get to show clients that they understand them, to show clients that they have identified their interests and to show clients that they can add value (not cost) by meeting those interests through the expertise and services the firm can offer.

So, at the point of your triumph, drive home the advantage you have built up. Make your case and make it stick.

Linking results to performance

This whole section is about delivering on commitments. As we have seen, the act of delivery presents all sorts of opportunities. Create as many opportunities to deliver as possible.

Another example is found by once again referring back to the dispute with the I.T. supplier.

The law firm, during the course of pre-trial preparations, will have to do many things. Much of the time the lawyers will be working from the firm's offices, unseen and hardly given a second's thought by the client. Occasionally the firm will become more visible, in particular when it has to do much of the following:

- Take initial detailed instructions

- Prepare an outline plan describing the documents they will want to see and the potential witnesses they will want to interview

- Prepare a costs report and agree a budget

- Attend the offices of the client to capture documents

- Attend the offices of the client to interview witnesses

- Prepare witness statements and get them agreed

- Report regularly and periodically on progress

- Correspond with the lawyers for the I.T. supplier

- Arrange (possibly) for mediation or some form of structured negotiation to take place.

There will, of course be many other things to do, but each of the nine areas of action listed above is a commitment from the lawyer to the client. Each point can be framed as a commitment and each commitment then achieved can be reported to the client, building trust, building confidence and providing opportunities to create more value.

Too often lawyers seem to want to make their work mysterious; they seem to want to say to their clients, "Don't you go worrying your dear little heads about the detail; we'll see to all the complicated things; you just have to pay the bills"!

The trouble is that the law firms (or in-house teams) that do this miss the opportunity to demonstrate that they are delivering on tangible commitments, that they are effective and efficient and worthy of the bills (or salaries) that are linked to their performance.

Delivering on commitments gives a framework to evaluate performance and value. Commitments made and achieved are the visible results of effort and expertise that might otherwise go unseen.

Commitments made and then achieved build trust that in turn builds value for the lawyers, the law firm and the client, and that is a result really worth pursuing.

Summary

So, there you have it. The seven elements of principled negotiation as described by Professor Roger Fisher and applied by me to relationship management in the context of the lawyer, the law firm and the business client.

Fisher's model is an excellent framework to understanding where value can be created and added in any relationship in any circumstances. It has a relevancy and clarity that resonates in just about everything I have ever done in my professional career and, because the theory is borne out by practice, it allows everyone to understand why things have worked well, why some things have worked less well and therefore how to repeat successes and avoid repeating failures.

Understanding the interests of your clients, contacts, superiors, subordinates and colleagues is the place to start when building a service founded on principles of excellence and value. Understanding interests then leads to the creative element of problem solving, which in turn is underpinned by demonstrating credibility in all that we do.

From there we can begin to build relationships for the long term and devise strategies that deliver our message in ways that are appreciated by the recipients and not just the sender.

Finally we can set up the milestones and commitments that are visibly and demonstrably achieved, which then feed back through the seven elements to support communication, build relationships, establish credibility and meet the client's interests.

From here the process may begin again to form a virtuous circle of finding, creating and adding value to relationships with clients, within legal teams and within law firms.

All of this is better for the lawyer, better for the law firm and best of all for the client.

Chapter Seven

"The Fog of Knowledge"

Introduction

Section Two of this book is all about relationship management. In Chapter Five is set out the 'Perception Test' with an analysis of different results from lawyers in law firms, lawyers from in-house legal teams and their business clients. This is so important because understanding the client's perception is a vital element of relationship management and, as we saw, by understanding generally how our words and actions may be perceived by everyone around us, not just clients, we put ourselves in a position to create and add value.

In Chapter Six described a preferred model for successful relationship management, based on the work of Professor Roger Fisher at Harvard Law School on *principled negotiation* and described to great effect in his book 'Getting to Yes'.

The next two chapters will explore two more ideas of how relationship management influences legal work. The first is christened a little bizarrely 'The Fog of Knowledge'; the second, more prosaically, is called 'Relationship Management and the effect on Risk and Value'.

'The Fog of Knowledge' is a phrase to describe the primeval soup of all the world's problems, issues, resources and solutions. It is the amorphic mass of knotted and interrelated questions and answers.

The role of the problem solver is to untie the knots to reveal the answers to the questions.

The fog of knowledge is represented by a circle. *(see fig. 1 overleaf)*

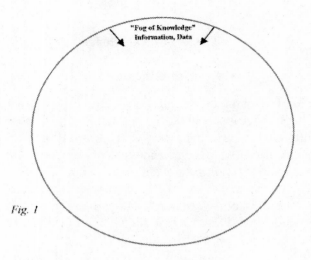

Fig. 1

We recognise the concept of the fog of knowledge because it is every personal and professional problem we have ever faced. We also know that every problem has an answer (indeed most problems have several answers), but what we do not always know is where to find the answer. The answer, however, is out there, somewhere in the fog of knowledge.

Businesses experience a close, if irritable and sometimes barely tolerated, relationship with the fog of knowledge on virtually a daily basis.

This is because businesses are equipped, usually, to make and (or) sell their product with considerable skill and expertise. They know their materials, their processes and their markets better than anyone else. What they are not equipped to deal with so well (and why should they be?) are all the related issues that have to be addressed because they are in business:

- Employees and Human Resources issues

- Supplier contracts

- Information Technology

- Tax
- Regulations
- Product liability
- Disputes
- Intellectual property
- Corporate governance
- Risk management

All of these issues, at some point, will need the help of people who are generally unconnected with the core activities of the business but who can unravel the knots and disperse the fog to reveal some of the answers.

These people are lawyers. Sometimes they are in-house, sometimes within law firms, but, wherever they are, they are the people who hold the fog lamps that can show the way.

These people are represented by a second circle.

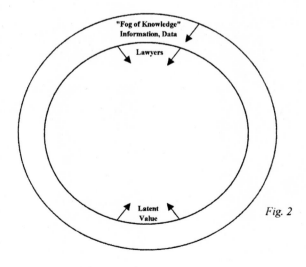

Fig. 2

Lawyers are equipped to find the answers. Their expertise and know-how represents what I have called *latent value* to the businesses they might be working for.

A significant question to be answered by lawyers, however, is why businesses should ask them to help solve their problems, in preference to other professional advisers or to finding self-help solutions.

Lawyers have no automatic right to be the problem solvers for businesses and simply claiming expertise is clearly insufficient. Where once lawyers might have been expected to be the first (even the only) people to be asked to help a business with its problems, now there are accountants, institutions, consultants and specialist businesses, who all have opportunities to sell their services too.

Lawyers, therefore, have to compete and lawyers have to demonstrate that their service is better than the service of their competitors. Lawyers might once have thrived by simply occupying the second ring, now they must do more. Their latent value must be turned into something else because lawyers who simply profess expertise can provide little meaningful help to any business that is fumbling around in the fog.

Of all the law firms that have ever pitched for work on the basis that they had expertise in a particular area how many have ever thought why the prospective client looked at them wearing a 'So what?' face? Now they know. Expertise by itself does not even get a law firm to first base.

The third ring *(See fig. 3 overleaf)*, therefore, represents the application of expertise. This I call *potential value* and it is much more important than latent value.

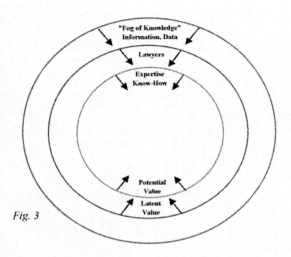

Fig. 3

Potential value is derived from the fact that lawyers have the expertise, or the tool kit, to solve problems. The value element however is in how they apply these skills on behalf of particular clients and particular problems.

Earlier chapters described the skills that lawyers possess and how they must maximise the potential their skills provide to create and add value for businesses and for themselves.

The skilled application of expertise overlaps with the Fisher model described above. It is about understanding interests and generating solutions that are relevant and useful to the client.

Remember competitive advantage comes from having such a detailed understanding of both the problem and the business that the solution is specifically developed to have immediate and practical benefits. This is why I have been such an advocate of the value to businesses of employing their own in-house lawyers.

It is their unique advantage over any other lawyer that allows them to both see the problems more clearly and to devise the solutions for their clients more empathetically. It is also a key learning point for all lawyers in law firms. Whether your clients have in-house lawyers or not, the closer you are able to align yourself to the interests of your client the better you will apply your expertise and know-how and the more potential value you will create both for yourself, your firm and for your client.

Lawyers who can apply their skills to give such advice or to find such solutions are indeed very valuable, but I have only described this as *potential value* for a very good reason. The most important circle, where *real value* is created and added, is in the fourth ring; Delivery.

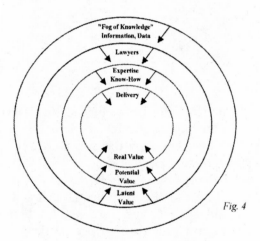

Fig. 4

It is the delivery of the advice (or the solution) when potential value is realised and the worth of the expertise and the efforts made on behalf of the client become tangible.

Again there are echoes with Fisher's seven elements to principled negotiation. In the notion of *delivery* are the relationship building, communication strategy and commitment stages of his model.

Here too there is confirmation of the finding of the Perception Test that businesses need solutions they can use. In

110

other words solutions that are relevant and timely; it also means solutions that are tailor-made and packaged for the people that have to understand and apply them.

The 'bulls-eye' of the concentric rings is the 'decision' the client makes, based on the advice received, or the application of the solution that is proposed.

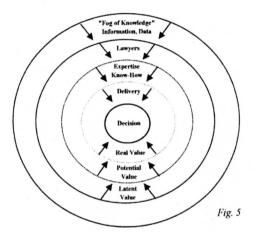

Fig. 5

What we can see from *Fig. 5* is the application of a relationship management model to demonstrate where different types of value may lie.

This is important because it helps to focus our minds on the type of lawyer we want to be, what skills we need to develop and how we should prioritise the training and management regimes that figure so prominently in both law firms and in-house legal teams.

For example, how often do we attend or send others on training courses to improve legal expertise? Certainly the vast majority of courses that are advertised and publicised are simply on legal subjects (such as the Human Rights Act, Data

Protection, Advanced Litigation etc). Are we doing these types of courses as part of a systematic development programme designed to improve the performance and value of ourselves and our lawyers? Or are we more usually chasing continuing professional development (CPD) hours and trying to find something, anything, of relevance?

There is a suspicion that for many it is the latter.

These courses are important and it should be recognised that building subject expertise represents only *latent value* to a law firm, legal team or (most importantly of all) to the client.

Consider how much less time is spent in training lawyers to apply their expertise and knowledge. Certainly no one ever told me that I should seek training in this area. No one suggested that I should try to find a mentor to teach me how he or she applied his or her knowledge, and yet it is here that *potential value* can be built up and developed.

More alarmingly even less time is given to training lawyers with the skills to actually deliver their advice and their solutions.

Lawyers need, as an absolute imperative, training in the communication skills and in the relationship skills that will allow them to turn *potential value* into *real value*.

Lawyers should be highly paid, well-respected and positive contributors to the business world. Many are already, but what seems clear is that our focus, as a profession, has been wrong. We seem to have become stuck with the notion that we should be experts in the law first and foremost. Actually what we need are lawyers who are excellent communicators and creative problem solvers, first and foremost.

During the course of researching this book, I travelled throughout the county to meet some of the best and brightest in-house lawyers. All without exception described how their client companies valued their contribution because the advice they gave was delivered in a manner that the client could use.

The Perception Test suggested that delivery was more important than content and while it cannot be said that content is not important, lawyers everywhere have got to get to grips with the idea that what they say is not as important as how they say it.

If you are a trainee being shown today how your law firm prefers to communicate with its clients, please ask the question 'But how do our clients like us to communicate with them?' If you are a senior lawyer, in-house or in a law firm, please listen to what your clients want.

Value is derived from the clients' requirements, not from the lawyers' preferences.

And if you are a cynic of any age or experience thinking that all this is very well, but you have P.I. insurers to look after, just ask yourself how many times clients have ever sued your firm because they clearly understood the advice they were given or because they were able to straightforwardly implement the solution that was proposed.

Value is created and added at the point of delivery.

Let us not get too hung up on whether it is Section 123 of the Law of Property Act or Section 321 of the Companies Act that is all-important. We must get the answer right, of course, but let us instead make the point of delivery of our expertise the real point of focus of our training and development.

It is what our clients want and it is what our competitors will give them if we do not.

Chapter Eight

Relationship management and the effect on risk and value

A book about relationship management is always open to the criticism of being only about "airy-fairy" matters unconnected with the real world.

The analysis of the Perception Test and the subsequent description of the preferred relationship management model have gone some way to dispelling that idea. The last chapter focused our attention on where value truly lies. In my world (real or otherwise!) real value lies more in the relationship skills of the lawyer than it does in their legal skills.

To illustrate this further another aspect of 'value' is described, this time in relation to the value of work (be it a corporate transaction, a contract to negotiate, litigation or whatever). I want to consider the link between "value" and "risk", and then to make some comments on the effect relationship management may have on both risk and value.

Fig. 6 (below) is a simple representation of the relationship between risk and value with 'risk' on the vertical axis and "value" along the horizontal axis. In general terms the higher the value a piece of work has the more risk there is attached to it. (For example, a transforming corporate deal involving a multi jurisdictional takeover by one global business of another global business carries huge value and enormous risk).

Risk Value Relationship

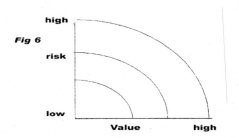

115

It is perfectly possibly to have a high value, low risk transaction (such as buying ten thousand standard personal computers for a new head office building) or a high risk, low value transaction (such as making circuit boards for electronic points systems on our railways).

In *Figs. 7, 8 and 9 (below)* three different aspects of legal work are superimposed on the graph:

- First, how the work is done
- Then by whom the work is done
- Finally when the work is done

The following analysis is based on my discussions with leading in-house lawyers and senior lawyers in law firms.

First, *Fig. 7*. Here it is proposed that as the type of work in question increases in risk and value, then so the way the work is done will change too. From the perspective of the in-house lawyer this ranges from outsourced senior teams, where risk and value are at their greatest, to unsupervised juniors where risk and value are much less significant.

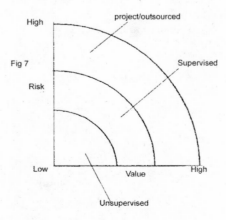

Risk Value Relationship

How is it done?

110

In the outside band, the work may well be outsourced to a law firm. This is not necessarily a reflection of the skills and expertise of the in-house lawyer, but will more likely reflect the fact that the work is going to be resource hungry requiring more pairs of hands than will be routinely available in-house. It is also, frankly, good risk management to occasionally put some strategic risk off-site. Another distinction here is that the reporting line to the business in these cases may well be at board level.

Within the law firm this type of 'outside band' work is most likely going to be completed by a team of lawyers rather than an individual (however talented) and most of the team will be very experienced practitioners.

The 'middle band' work, if it is done in-house and not outsourced, will most probably be the responsibility of a senior or experienced lawyer (possibly working within a small legal team) but almost certainly as part of a larger multi-disciplinary project team drawn from different area of the business. If more junior lawyers are involved, they will almost certainly be closely supervised.

If this is work being done in a law firm, it is probably under the control of a senior associate or junior partner. It is less likely that there will be a team of lawyers involved. The reporting line to the business, however, will be at a senior level though probably not at board level.

For work in the inner band, both for in-house lawyers and lawyers in law firms, these are tasks for unsupervised juniors. Indeed, in-house this may be work that is considered to be so low risk as to be left within business teams to simply 'take a view'. If there is a reporting line, it is likely to be managed at a suitably junior level as well.

In *Fig. 8 (overleaf)*, the graph now shows not 'how' the work is done but who is most likely to be doing it. As already mentioned with regard to *Fig 7*, it is invariably the case that the more junior lawyers will be doing the work that carries less risk or is of a low value, while the more senior and experienced lawyers will ply their trade in the areas where risk and value are most significant.

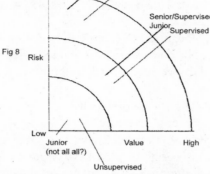

Risk Value Relationship

How is it done? Who does it?

Fig 8

Fig. 9 reveals a time-line regarding when work is completed in terms of the priority it is given. There are no surprises here either; as you can see, the work attracting the most risk or the highest value is given the greatest priority. On the other hand, work of low risk and value is given the least priority.

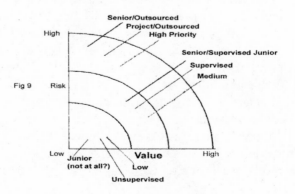

Risk Value Relationship

How is done? Who does it? When is it done?

Fig 9

118

What do these graphs tell us?

At first glance, they probably only confirm obvious things, such as the fact that in-house lawyers and lawyers in law firms tend to look at work in a predictable way. If it is high risk or high value, the better, more experienced lawyers are going to be doing it, probably in teams and probably with a greater sense of priority than less valuable or lower risk work.

What is interesting is the way that managing relationship can impact on these admittedly predictable models.

Two areas of risk, for example, are first whether the lawyers involved are close enough to their client to understand the client's interests and second whether they are competent enough, in terms of expertise and experience, to do the job.

If the relationship between client and lawyer is new, the client's interests are less obvious and so what tends to happen is that law firms overcompensate for this risk and put forward lawyers with greater experience than is needed and possibly more lawyers than are needed as well.

While this is in one sense an understandable reaction, it has unfortunate consequences because it means that the client is either effectively overcharged for the real value of the work or the law firms must cut back dramatically on their margins, even to the point of making an economic loss.

Worse still is what happens when established relationships begin to fail between lawyers and their clients. Again what happens is that more senior lawyers (sometimes increased numbers of lawyers) are brought in to reassure the client or to rescue a file. The effect however is to have work done less productively than should be the case. The cost in these circumstances is more likely to be borne by the law firm, but it is nevertheless inefficient from the clients' perspective as well and clearly very destructive of value.

Lawyers in these situations often really resent this scenario developing as they see profits eroded to nothing, but that resentment can often further spoil the relationship and perpetuate the problem. It becomes, to coin a phrase, a 'lose-lose'! *Fig. 10* therefore shows in a very stark way that bad

119

relationships (and to a slightly lesser extent, new relationships) have the effect of pulling low risk work into higher risk

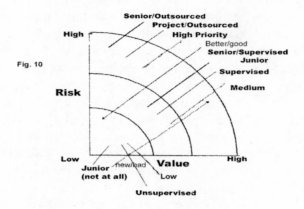

categories and therefore increasing costs to both lawyers and clients.

Importantly, however, the converse is also true. The sooner new relationships are established and the better those relationships are managed, the greater the reduction in the risks associated with the way that work is handled.

In these circumstances the effect is to allow work to be done by the appropriately qualified lawyers and even, on occasions, by less experienced lawyers than may first be considered necessary. If trust and confidence are not in doubt, then work can be managed with a healthy margin and to the clients' economic benefit as well. Looking again at the graphs, work is effectively pulled back into a lower risk band to everyone's benefit.

Another economic advantage of improving relationships is the fact that lawyers are better able to resist predatory attacks from competitors. Apart from the psychological 'feel good'

120

factors, good relationships mean more scope for the lawyers to manage margins and should mean, therefore, that it is easier to resist the threat of competitors pinching work by undercutting the cost of legal services.

Effectively the new suitors of a client, attempting to woo it away with promises of fabulous legal services, have to pitch on the tightest of margins. So, unless their cost control is superb (not something I have particularly noticed about law firms, I have to say) they will be taking a big gamble on the number of lawyers they commit to a deal and their relative experience.

This is probably the biggest reason why new relationships fail. The sums are not done properly, or are done but ignored, and the relationship suffers because the law firm realises it will either have an economic failure or a dissatisfied client, or both.

If any firm is threatened with losing an established client to a competitor firm beating it on price, one of three things is probably true:

- The existing relationship is not well managed, or

- If the relationship is good, the lawyers have not shared the economic benefit of their wider margin with the client, or

- If the relationship is good the law firm's cost control is not good enough.

The simple fact is that improving relationships improves profitability; worsening relationships risks lower profits, even losses. Good relationships and good relationship management therefore have a significant economic impact and should not be ignored in any circumstances at all.

A similar point can also be made when considering 'when' work is done.

If the relationship between lawyer and client is recognised to be poor, the temptation for the lawyer is to rush to complete work to show the commitment that was perceived to have been lacking and to rebuild that which has broken down. Completing work in advance of when is actually necessary, however, carries obvious costs to the lawyer. Those costs hit the bottom line. But good relationships permit work to be done according to when it should be done, ensuring that margins and workflows are effectively and efficiently managed.

Considering how work is done, by whom it is done and when it is done, well-managed relationships improve the profitability of the law firm and reduce costs for the client, whereas poor relationships have the effect of reducing the profitability of lawyers (even tipping them into losses) while increasing costs for the client.

Win-win or lose-lose, relationship management is not warm, fluffy airy-fairy psycho-babble; it is hard nosed, cold light of day, harsh economic reality.

Chapter Nine

Case studies

Although much of this book is based on my own experiences and observations, I have also been very fortunate to have had the opportunity to meet a number of senior in-house lawyers and lawyers from law firms. The three case studies discussed in the following pages are based on real situations, but brought together as a hypothetical amalgam of the shared experiences of many of us. I am sure there will be issues that are very familiar to you too.

My purpose is to illustrate that the ideas and principles described in earlier chapters of the book can have practical application. The exercise also seeks to demonstrate that 'hope', frankly, is not a strategy that can be relied upon. It is almost always better to have a plan than it is to simply hope that efforts will be appreciated and value will be seen.

Case Study no 1

Ben McCarthy joined ABC Bank three months ago. He is the new Marketing Director for all retail products, both savings and loans. His background is in clothing where he made his name producing high profile and controversial TV advertisements. He is incredibly ambitious and wants to put ABC Bank 'on the map'. Just before Ben joined the bank, the then Head of Legal and Regulatory Affairs, Jeremy Pate, left the company to join a small market town general practice. The suspicion was, although nothing had been said officially, that he had lost touch with the ambitions of the bank, which itself had seen dramatic growth in the last five years. Jeremy was liked, but was seen very much as 'old school'. He was a thoroughly decent and nice man who was also a skilled technical lawyer; he had served on a number of industry sponsored task forces and was well known for his cautious, some said 'whiter than white' approach. Ben has just been given board approval for an ambitious and aggressive marketing campaign. The intention is to target competitor products, exceed the deal offered by the competitor and grab as much market share as possible. The board are enthusiastic and see this particular initiative as a means of meeting year-end targets and leap-frogging their closest rival when year-end figures are announced. You have just been appointed the new Head of Legal and Regulatory Affairs. You have a meeting with Ben later in the week as part of the general round of introductory meetings. You are aware of Ben's reputation, a fact underlined by the email you received from him this morning. It said: "Look forward to meeting you on Friday. Hope we won't take too long though, as I am signing off agency work for the new campaign later that day. No need for you to be involved. Your predecessor was a bit of an old woman, wouldn't let anything go. Since I joined we self certify and, surprise surprise, the thought police are not banging at the door. Much better. Look forward to our chat. Regards. Ben."

So, what is to be done?

Aggression and arrogance are sometimes seen as the preserve of the legal profession rather than our clients, but here we are with a new head of legal and a very assertive client.

Common sense suggests that it would be a mistake to go into battle just yet, certainly while the new man in charge of marketing has the board entranced and while the new head of legal has yet to establish her own credibility.

Let us first try to identify the key interests at stake.

- ABC Bank, in this instance, has two obvious interests. First it wants to be successful, sell more product and beat up its competitors. Second it wants to run its business within the law enhancing its reputation as a reliable and secure institution.

- Ben's interests are to justify the board's faith in him, his salary and to live up to his reputation. It will, however,

124

not be in Ben's interests to appear in court as the guy responsible for the biggest OFT investigation in years.

- The new head of legal has interests too. She wants to establish her credentials as someone who can add value, who can be trusted, who has a commercial focus and who will, when necessary say 'no' to protect her client and its reputation.

Even from these three brief paragraphs it is clear that there are more interests that coincide than diverge. There is an awful lot of bluster about Ben's email but in truth he will not want to make an enemy of the senior in-house lawyer. If the board have done their job properly, they will not have hired a total lunatic and he will be a bright (if brash) guy with his head screwed on.

If we have noted the various interests correctly, it is actually perfectly possible to read Ben's email in an entirely different way. Adjusted to remove the arrogance it simply says:

"Looking forward to seeing you, though a bit busy just now. Experimenting with a new sign off procedure that saves time and expense. If you are happy with it we can both get credit for improving the service. In the past we have been uncompetitive because we have tried to avoid all risks."

If this had been Ben's email it is hard to see where the objection would be. By identifying the interests we also identify common ground; by removing some of the emotive language we can also deal with the real issues.

Too often we get stuck with how to deal with personalities rather than issues. 'So-and-so can be really awkward.' 'I don't like him, he's always unreasonable' etc. If we find options that can be seen to meet people's interests and which are credible, it is much harder for them to be awkward and unreasonable. It does not necessarily make it more pleasant to deal with them, but it probably makes getting your job done a little bit easier.

If Ben proves to be a more difficult customer than at first appears, the new head of legal will have to think again. There is enough common ground, however, for her to build on.

Case Study no 2

In Case Study no 1, the issue was relatively straightforward. Case Study no 2 is much more complex.

You are the Head of Legal and Regulatory Affairs at ABC Bank. You have been in this position for some time now and your team of three are stable and work well together. You have been with the bank for ten years, becoming the Head of Legal two years ago. Your team consists of Mary, who has also been with the bank for ten years and who is your effective deputy, Simon, a legal executive who has been with the bank for longer than anyone can remember, and John, who is two years qualified and in his first job after completing a training contract with one of the larger city law firms.

The work is generally interesting, but fits a relatively routine pattern. Morale is okay and there are no particular management issues save for the fact that everyone is incredibly busy. While variety is not a feature of the work, volume certainly is and with the generic growth in the bank the team feels under pressure all of the time.

At the last Head Office managers meeting you were told that there was to be a recruitment freeze for the next six months at least. The team accepted the news with resignation, but you know that it is getting tougher to keep it all together.

Then, out of the blue, the board announce a new joint venture with a world-renowned credit card company that will allow ABC Bank to run several different affinity credit card schemes. All the deals will be offered, processed and administered via the Internet. There is a great deal of very positive press coverage and the share price rises to a two year high on the back of the announcement. It is the first time any bank in the UK has embarked on such an ambitious scheme and everyone in the bank is talking about it.

You then receive a memo from the Sales Director: "Following yesterday's announcement, please consider and report what legal resources will be needed and an approximate budget for the preparatory work. The board assumes you will use a known city law firm. This is a project that must not be delayed."

You know that this is just the sort of opportunity that your team would love to be involved in, but you are also concerned that they have just too much to do already. It will be incredibly expensive to outsource all the work and that annoys you too when you cannot recruit but have at least some of the relevant expertise in-house. You also know that if the work is outsourced, morale will go through the floor. If any service levels fall, the ABC Bank are never slow to criticise.

This is a real tough one, but again let us start with looking at the interests at stake.

- ABC Bank has just agreed a strategically significant deal that has already added shareholder value and is in the public domain. But cost is a factor as well. The recruitment freeze suggests a degree of belt tightening that will make large legal bills less than welcome.

- The ego of the CEO will not want to be dented by any failure or hitch; delay has already been flagged as a risk.

- Your team are loyal, but feel taken for granted. If all this work is outsourced, even though they are too busy to do it now, they will feel that they are not trusted with a big project either.

- If anyone in the team should leave, or even 'go off the boil', service levels will drop and the bank will suffer as well.

I think the key to sorting this situation out is balance.

The strategic, high profile nature of the tie up suggests it is a deal high in value and high in risk. It calls for a good deal of experience and that experience will not be in-house. It must be right, therefore, for the essence of the deal to be outsourced. This, however, brings into play the interests of the law firm.

- The law firm will want some public and professional recognition, to make a healthy profit and to enhance its reputation.

The law firm is going to need access, information and clear direction. It will not want any obfuscation or to be denied information it thinks will be relevant. The law firm, in short, needs the in-house function to be firmly on its side.

What is beginning to emerge is a set of circumstances where mutual interests can be identified:

- The bank recognises the need to spend money on legal resources to avoid damage to the deal and its reputation. (This also has long term benefits for the in-house team and should be utilised in future resources negotiations.)

- The law firm needs the in-house team to avoid damage to the deal and to its reputation.

- The in-house team have their best opportunity for some time to show key players in the bank why they are important and valuable.

When the budgets are put together, I am sure that a significant liaison role will emerge for the in-house team. They will also be able to take on some of the non-core legal work, for example with regard to the customer documentation for the credit cards, marketing materials and contract management.

In addition, the in-house team also have an opportunity to build a case that demonstrably saves the bank money on external legal fees if the in-house team share some of the legal work with the law firm. If this is handled successfully, it may even be possible to leverage this benefit and agree to some additional recruitment, lifting the freeze and alleviating some of the on-going pressure.

Finally the tender process to select the right law firm might also require some in-house training to help share the expertise required for such transactions with a view to saving more costs next time round.

If the plan comes together:

- The bank will have the level of legal support and risk management it requires;

- The law firm will have the profile and the fee income it wants while getting clear and timely instructions;

- The in-house team will raise their profile with their directors, develop some new skills, be involved in a strategically significant project and get some long-term support.

In some situations the plan will not come together, but that almost is not the point. Faced with a difficult problem and the very real possibility of significant damage to the morale and effectiveness of the legal team, it is possible to plan a way forward. As mentioned elsewhere, 'hope' is not the strategy of choice.

Identifying the interests of each group reveals a great deal of common ground. This in turn allows for different options to emerge; options that do not demand conflict but which can actually bring the groups closer together than they would have been in the absence of the problem.

What is then needed of course, as we have seen, is for the communication strategy to work to put into effect the preferred plan. The communication strategy in this case needs to be with the bank's directors, with the team and with the law firm. A slightly different tone, with perhaps a different emphasis, will be needed in each case.

Consideration should also be given to the BATNA in each case, because each of the interest groups represents a different negotiation and a different relationship to manage.

Clearly all seven elements of the relationship management model apply. I use this case study in my workshops and, as in most situations, there are several acceptable solutions. The key to unlocking any solution, however, is to follow the framework and then let your own skill, experience and creativity find the solution that works best for you.

Case Study no 3

This is perhaps the most difficult case study. Again it is based on the real stories of real in-house lawyers given to me during the course of my research. It will strike a chord with many in-house lawyers who will perhaps recognise elements of their own teams. It will also be of interest to those lawyers who work in private practice and will help them to understand that there are many more pressures on an in-house legal team than simply getting on with the legal work.

You are the Head of Legal and Regulatory affairs for ABC Bank. Your team consists of ten lawyers. Ted and Sarah are ten years qualified and manage two teams of four. Ted's team consists of Jill and Robert (both 3-5 years qualified), Sam, newly qualified, and Justin, who is a paralegal. Sarah's team includes Paul, who is four years qualified, Kathy and Bill, who are legal executives of many years' experience, and Brian, who is a trainee. You have a number of management issues to address.

Robert has never been a high achiever, but is fairly stable and performs to the competency standards expected. He is, however, one of life's whingers. Nothing is ever right; business contacts are unreasonable in their demands only to him; his PC is the slowest in the department and his annual holiday is usually a disaster due to the ineffectual staff that work in every hotel he stays in. He is recently divorced and now wants a pay rise (which he says is long overdue) partly, you suspect, because he has to buy a second home to move into. The team have had a grudging regard for Robert in the past, but you now suspect that he is affecting morale.

Jill and Paul on the other hand are star performers and much of the success of the team is due to their open commercial style. They are also very good lawyers. Ted, however, has told you that both have had approaches from the Jujitsu Bank, which has moved head office twenty miles down the road. Jujitsu recently hit the legal press for paying 20% more than London rates to attract their first in-house legal team. There is no way ABC Bank will compete with them on salary.

You are particularly concerned because the depth of experience in the team is not there to cover for such a possible loss of expertise. The less experienced in the team are good, but need more training and do not yet have the full confidence of the business managers they come across.

Finally, you have recently received the following email from the Finance Director: "As part of the drive to reduce costs in real terms year on year, please report on your progress to date for the current financial year. I note that despite maintaining a static headcount figure legal costs have increased by 25% to nearly £3m. I assume this increase is largely due to greater outsourcing, but it is a significant concern and must be addressed."

The increase in outsourcing costs is largely accounted for by three high profile court cases in which the bank has been sued for reneging on I.T. contracts where budgets had overrun and delivery dates had been missed. You currently use six medium sized law firms, whom Kathy spends most of her day chasing for one thing or another.

In my own experience, and in that of many of the people I have met, some of these issues are very familiar indeed.

- How do you bring round under-performing or negative staff?

- How do you give meaningful careers to ambitious people?

131

- How do you plan for the eventuality of key staff leaving?

- How do you manage down costs and improve the quality of a service?

- How should you organise outsourced work?

Again, I believe the place to start is in identifying interests. Take Robert for example.

Here the interests include those of the head of legal, who has to manage a "high maintenance" individual. Robert is also a potential burden in the team in respect of your attempts to build a cohesive sense of team spirit and he is someone who may negatively influence the business contacts you are trying to impress within the company.

There are the interests of Robert's colleagues. It is hard work having someone around who is always negative and it does tend to knock everyone's productivity. There are also the interests of Robert's clients who may be put off using him. Finally there are Robert's interests. He is clearly a troubled man.

If you fail to manage this situation and Robert is seen to 'get away' with poor and disruptive performance, the head of legal's position is undermined. If the reaction from you is perceived to be excessive, not only do you leave yourself open to a possible claim, but team building is also significantly damaged.

So, what are the options?

In the first place we know that Robert thinks he is long overdue a pay rise. If we separate the personality from the issue, this is obviously a matter that should be addressed. We should review the position, make sure our own actions have credibility and not 'penalise' Robert because of his manner.

That said, his manner must also improve and, hard though it is, he must be tackled on why his attitude appears to be so negative. Often a negative attitude has not been addressed. Over time the negativity worsens and the behaviour becomes even harder to deal with to the point where productivity in the team slides alarmingly and good people leave.

It is almost like having a disruptive child in the classroom. Of course the head of legal must act fairly and credibly, but in the worst cases the errant child has to be expelled to preserve an appropriate environment for everyone else.

More bad news is in the possibility of losing your star performers. Will Jill and Paul leave for the extra money they may get elsewhere?

Clearly you cannot (not usually anyway) magic up an extra 20% on salary. Even if you could it may not have the desired effect; indeed it might be more trouble than it is worth. Jill and Paul may feel you have kept them at an artificially low level and what about the other team members as well?

At the risk of getting boring, check out their interests.

First, people rarely leave an environment they enjoy just for money. Trading good work, thoughtful management and friendly colleagues for all the uncertainties of an entirely new regime and an extra 20% (less tax) is not necessarily a good career move.

People leave jobs either because they are unhappy or because they can move to a bigger role where their ambitions can be fulfilled more readily. Money is a secondary, even tertiary, factor.

It is however also the case that people will from time to time move on and it will not always be possible to retain staff you want to keep. The balance to be struck, I think, is to try and ensure that people do not leave because of something you could have done or should have done but didn't do.

What are the development plans for Jill and Paul? What are their career objectives and how can you help fulfil them? These are the key issues for staff. Care about their development and they are much less likely to leave.

Money may be an issue, but it probably won't be the only reason they leave; however, if they leave, hopefully they will go with positive thoughts about the business and the legal team. They will always be, potentially at least, 'brand advocates' for you and the bank, so you should always encourage their success and be grateful you were able to keep them for as long as you did.

That still leaves a gaping hole in the team, however, and a hole that has to be filled. There is not usually a satisfactory quick fix. The problem, however, can be managed with a long-term approach.

No one individual should be allowed to become indispensable. If your team were a computer system that crashed irreparably because one screen failed to work on the network, you would be understandably unimpressed with the supplier. The watchword is 'resilience'. Your team, like your computer system, should be resilient enough to withstand a component failure.

You have junior staff and their development plans should involve an element of being able to back up team members. You also have an external panel of law firms and here too is a resource that should be familiar enough with the work of the in-house team to be able to lend emergency support that is not disruptive to the business of the bank.

The other major problem you have is trying to manage down costs while improving service. This is a holy grail, one to be pursued! Part of the answer, in this case, is to stop the problem at source. I.T. contracts generally go wrong because of supplier's failure to deliver what the client wanted or because of the client's failure to articulate what it wanted (or a combination of the two).

In most cases the absence of a record of what was agreed highlights the subsequent issues of contention. If the in-house team can help support the I.T. or procurement functions to get the initial stages right, it is less likely that litigation will follow at a later stage. I know it sounds like an obvious point but it does not happen in surprisingly many cases.

Faced with what might seem like an overwhelming litigation burden, the in-house team might be forgiven for making a case to recruit additional litigation support. While this may provide temporary respite in the legal department, it does not address the underlying problems. When the levels of litigation are back under proper management it may also mean that the team is then over-resourced.

The smarter approach would be to recruit additional contract, regulatory or compliance support and solve the fundamental fault. It may take longer to get to the solution, but the solution will be far more efficient and cost effective for the business.

The outsourcing issue identified is also common one and will be addressed later. For now though we have a situation in the case study where six firms are engaged and require the support of one full time member of your team.

The question that should be asked is whether six firms are too many?

There may well be benefits to reducing the number to three or four firms. Potential advantages are first the greater bargaining/purchasing power you may create, second the added value that may come from being closer to fewer firms and third you potentially release Kathy from a rather unfulfilling role and immediately create additional internal resource at no extra cost.

Summary conclusions from the three case studies

It is easy and trite to write a few paragraphs on a case study and present solutions that in the real world may take months to implement (if they can be implemented at all).

It is not my intention to present these three case studies as having straightforward model answers. It is my intention, however, to underline the recuring themes in this book.

- First: every situation should be managed and not left to chance, even when that means making a conscious decision to do nothing.

- Second; the best framework for managing situations like these is the Fisher model of identifying interests, dealing with issues not personalities and selecting solutions that meet as many of the identified interests as you can.

This section has covered various aspects of relationship management that are absolutely crucial to creating and realising value, whether you are an in-house lawyer or in private practice.

SECTION THREE

Chapter Ten

Opportunities for improving value, the law firms

There is a danger that the following section will appear to be an almighty rant about law firms and the way legal services are delivered.

I will therefore start with three statements I genuinely believe to be true;

- Law firms in the United Kingdom are the best in the world.

- The level of legal expertise available to corporate clients in this country is second to none.

- Lawyers in this country are some of the hardest working, most dedicated and talented people you will find in any profession.

Professor Fisher says that the word 'but' in negotiations acts as the great eraser, wiping out everything said before it as if it had not been said at all.

For example, "Yes of course I am happy for your mother to stay with us indefinitely, but..." or "Yes I would love to help with the carnival committee, but..." or, perhaps most common of all "It's not that I am afraid of commitment, but marriage is a big step to take when we have only known each other for a few years".

Knowing, therefore, the effect of the word 'but' it is necessary to repeat my high regard for lawyers, despite the criticisms set out in the following pages!

Because there is so much talent in the profession the service should and could be even better. There is little doubt in my mind that this is the case. The lawyers and law firms in this country are sometimes successful despite their systems, processing and cultures, not because of them.

The main areas of weakness are;

• Costs, costs and costs. Let us call this the billing issue.

• It is also regrettably the case that too many remain arrogant; it is difficult to understand the macho culture of the deal room where the deal is only signed off at the end of an all night negotiation. It is inefficient, frighteningly expensive and obviously damaging to family life. This is the big boys' issue.

• Another alarming gap in the law firm's credibility is the lack of cost management. This is both in terms of what the client is billed and the control of the firm's own overheads. On occasions it is frankly absolutely woeful. This is the lack of control issue.

• Furthermore, law firms often lack a commercial focus. They often fail miserably to interpret their clients' wishes, are very poor at selling anything at all and they are, it seems, genetically modified to be resistant to change. This is the stuck in the mud issue.

• Finally, but by no means of least significance, there are still far too few women in senior positions and young recruits are treated often like so much cannon fodder. This is the management issue.

Apart from that they are not too bad.

The billing issue

The position is summed up in the issue of billing. This may be repetition but (that word again) can you honestly think of any other purchase decision that is made on the basis of an uncertain outcome, an uncertain price and an uncertain incidence of when the price has to be paid?

It is absolutely ridiculous. Here we are, in an age when technology is so sophisticated that it can support a multi-jurisdictional, multi-currency, global business from a windswept Scottish croft. Yet international law firms, in their glitzy city marbled cathedrals to capitalism, are using the same method of billing as that used by their founding fathers whose names remain on the law firms' letterheads.

The lack of innovation in this area is an appalling indictment of the institutional arrogance of law firms. They know that their clients continually complain about this one issue above all others and yet they still have done so little to address it. It is not, I am quite sure, that they lack integrity or honesty, but, if that is not the case, then they do stand accused of being both arrogant and complacent.

There is little doubt that the day will come (maybe in five years, maybe in ten) when corporate clients will buy commoditised legal services in the same way we now buy car insurance. They will log onto some virtual brokerage as yet not invented. Let us call it www.LitigationDirectbid.com. Potential clients will answer a dozen or so pre-scripted questions and the site will then generate a fixed price, quality assured quotation, with a 'what happens next' report. And there will not have been a lawyer in sight.

Law firms today can get away with answering the question of 'what will it cost?' with a well-practised sorrowful shrug and a trust-me look. Not for much longer though; the alarm clock is already ringing and there are only so many times you can press the snooze button before it is too late to do anything about it.

The investment that has to be made is huge. Whole new systems must be built and historical data has to be modelled and manipulated to define the risk parameters. The most important people in the law firm of the future may be the IT developer, the director of finance and the equivalent of a litigation actuary predicting future trends by reference to past performance and results.

If the law firms do not make this investment, then as legal markets around the world become less regulated, the venture capitalists and the entrepreneurs of every shape and size will move in. They will develop new markets and create a new demand that only they will have the means to satisfy.

Law firms will then have no choice but to curl up and die.

There are firms who are seeking to develop new technology solutions, but the pace of change is not fast enough and this is partly due to the way law firms are organised.

The partnership principle may have been ideal in 1896, even in 1956, but it would not be invented today. It is cumbersome, inefficient, slow and conservative. It is risk averse, riddled with vested interests and unfocused. It would be like shareholders running plcs and it does not work. Despite the development of chief executives and the recognition that managing partner is not a position to be filled by the guy next to retire, there remains a significant lack of managerial expertise.

There are still major law firms that even today resemble a group of middle-aged sole practitioners working under the banner of a shared logo but with little interest in what is going on even two doors down their own corridor. They are going to go out of business in the next ten years unless they change out of all recognition.

Lawyers have got to accept that their survival (let alone their future success) depends on their ability to reinvent both themselves and their services.

We can see this by looking at the global accountancy firms. Whether it is through audit, accountancy, tax, regulatory compliance, corporate governance, risk management and (increasingly) legal services, they have repackaged themselves and their services to offer their clients commoditised products at transparent prices.

It is not that corporate clients necessarily want to deal with accountants in preference to lawyers. Nor is it that the lawyers were not able to do what the accountants have done. It is almost as if the lawyers did not realise that they were in a race. When the starting gun was fired, the accountants did not hang around to explain the rules of the game; instead they ran off into the far distance perhaps never to be caught again.

The irony is that every lawyer thinks that the accountancy firms have stolen a march on the law firms and every lawyer grumbles about it. It is like a playground tiff. 'But Sir, Jimmy didn't tell me it was a race; it's not fair.'

Well the message is this guys: It ain't going to get easier, because in a very short while there will be a lot more people in the race and none of them are going to do the law firms any favours at all!

The banks will do conveyancing when conveyancing becomes as easy as buying a new car. The roadside recovery organisations will do motor insurance litigation when court practice is computerised and standardised further. Corporate clients will demand fixed price deals on everything from technology contract negotiation to major commercial litigation. Trusted brands like Virgin and Tesco will exploit opportunities to package family law products on the back of wealth and lifestyle management, although the idea of a Virgin divorce may take a little selling, even for Richard Branson.

It is absurd and plainly wrong to think that in such a competitive, innovative and risk taking world, an old style partner in an old style law firm might still make a decent living by:

- Not returning telephone calls, or

- Writing incomprehensible letters, or

- Charging by the hour with no quality assurance and no certainty of outcome.

How can law firms respond to the billing issue?

First, they must be honest with their clients and with themselves. It is not good enough to say that their internal systems do not allow for innovative or fixed price billing. If Mr Ford had insisted that the only car he would ever make would be the Model T and the only colour it would ever be would be black, he might not be quite the businessman we remember

141

today. Yet once upon a time that was all his internal systems and processes allowed.

There is no short cut; there does need to be a massive investment in the structure, processes and systems of the modern law firm. It may be that regulatory change will help facilitate the changes that are needed. Access to capital is obviously a key requirement after all.

The first thing that has to change, however, is attitude.

The big boys issue

A while ago I had lunch with a senior partner in a very successful law firm. He told me that profitability was up by twenty percent, that turnover was up by forty percent and that he had drawn half a million in salary for the third year in a row. He was not convinced that his world was going to crash in around him and that it was all going to end in tears.

He was also on his third marriage, looked ten years older than the date on his birth certificate and had not had a whole week off all year. His world might not be in imminent danger of crashing around him, but he was certainly in danger of crashing around his world.

We have all had to put in the hours; we all know that hard work is a pre-requisite of a successful career. It is my view, however, that being over-weight, over-tired and over-stressed has nothing to do with quality legal services.

One in-house lawyer I spoke to asked a city lawyer whether he routinely worked through the night. "Absolutely!" came the emphatic reply. "Then I will not be instructing you," said the in-house director.

Until the culture of law firms change, until family friendly policies are implemented instead of just published, a great deal of talent will be wasted. Lawyers with more sense will lose career opportunities but at least they will keep their sanity.

If you were lucky enough to be able to afford a thoroughbred race horse, to have it trained by the best trainers and groomed for greatness, would you then run it for fourteen

142

hours a day without a break? Why then, do law firms treat their most precious assets like pit ponies?

It is wasteful and it is stupid.

The lack of control issue

In an hourly rate of say £400, what would be the amount of profit?

£200? £20? £2?

The law firm of five years ago would not have been the place to go for the answer. Today it is getting better, but it is not as good as it should be. There is a significant lack of precision in the way law firms manage the profitability of a transaction.

Ask a litigator for example at what point they can discount their overall bill and still make a profit and you will get a blank look. Yet every single day somewhere (probably many times over) there will be a conversation between lawyer and client in which the lawyer reduces the amount of the bill. Often by a very significant amount.

Two points arise. First; has the law firm made so much profit that it can effectively give away thousands of pounds and not worry? Second, is the law firm ultimately running an uneconomic file?

There are no obvious answers to these questions, but I am nervous about firms that can reduce their billing significantly. Either clients have been taken for a ride or they are not running a business where firms know their bottom line. Not good either way.

This also goes back to a point made earlier. Many non-law businesses actually thrive on their ability to manage their margin. Those firms that cannot compete in what will become a highly competitive market will either lose work or lose money, or both.

One in-house lawyer told how he had had a meeting with a partner in a law firm that wanted to renegotiate the standard fee per file for some bulk litigation. The problem for the law firm was that after six months of diligently processing the work, it did not think it would be able to make a profit.

143

It had previously won the work (which is traditionally, perhaps notoriously, very price sensitive) on the basis that it was able to undercut its competitors. However it now needed several pounds per case more. The in-house lawyer was told (in the most reasonable of terms) that if the fee did not go up, it was unlikely that the firm would be able to offer the same level of service.

As far as the law firm was concerned, this was all perfectly reasonable. It had a good, professional relationship with the client and this open and frank dialogue was all about good client care.

The client, however, did not quite see how this was at all in its interests. It promptly withdrew all instructions and placed the business with a competitor at the price the client was prepared to pay.

Many lawyers in law firms will think that the client has been arrogant and off hand. That may be right, but did the client have a choice?

The supplier of a service has told the customer that it cannot make a profit so the cost to the customer will go up. This is not an open and frank dialogue; it is a suicide note.

What should the law firm have done;

• First: it should not have bid for work without understanding that it was profitable work to bid for. Buying turnover is a strategy for amateurs, buying work that makes a loss is a strategy for lemmings.

• Second: the law firm should have first looked to reduce the overhead, not increase the price of the service.

After all, this is how most businesses work.

The message the law firm was giving was a simple one. We are so inefficient that we now require the client to underwrite the inefficiency. Neat if you can get away with it.

The work was rightly placed with a new firm that had its costs under control and could therefore offer the client a price it was prepared to pay and still make the profit it wanted.

It is not easy nor is it always fair. Law firms, however, have got to be able to compete not just with each other but also with other types of business. At present many are ill equipped to do so. Now is therefore the time to accelerate the pace of change.

The stuck in the mud issue

Most lawyers think that they have a commercial focus. This might be true compared with the law firms of a few years ago and it is also true that today the best law firms have a more commercial focus than some of their competitors. However, this is not the same as saying that they have really grasped what their clients want and it seems to me there is still a significant gap that ought to be closed between the commercial focus law firms give and the focus their clients would like them to give.

Of course there are and there should be limits to what law firms will say and how far they will go. It is, however, these limits that we need to explore further and in particular why they are justified by law firms but not liked by their clients.

Typically, law firms offer a number of reasons why they are constrained in the advice they give or the risk they are prepared to accept. These are matters such as:

- Systems constraints,

- Overbearing P.I. policies,

- Bad experiences with unreasonable or awkward clients, and

- Decision-making structures within their firms that are too long and too complicated.

This may sound harsh, but these four issues are mere excuses for the failure of lawyers to recognise that clients want much more from their legal advisers.

In individual circumstances there can always be found some justification for caution and restraint. It is not in every case that caution must be thrown aside or that all clients want to see a gung-ho attitude to risk taking. That is not the point, but in general law firms do not go far enough in helping to shape the strategies that will potentially deliver the extra value their clients would like to see. In general therefore the profession is failing the business world.

I do not pretend to have all the answers. It is not easy to state what actions should be taken. Sometimes the answer is not a matter of finding a specific solution. It is much more about a law firm's attitude and approach and here we are back to perception and reality issues.

That said, there is a clue as to what is required in an old Chinese proverb. It says quite simply, 'One cannot stand still in a moving river'.

Change is a constant, and constant change is a prerequisite of competitive advantage and therefore of success.

In a fast moving commercial setting the law firms that do not run at the pace of their clients do not see the world through their clients' eyes. It is so much harder to be sensitive to the client's perception of risk when left behind. This leads inevitably to a more cautious approach.

The more alive a law firm can be to the environment of its client, the more able it will be to appreciate the client's sense of risk in that environment. Innovation and development for law firms, therefore, is something that has to be tackled systematically and to be part of the culture of law firms on an ongoing basis. Change is a process, not an event.

This is not about having state-of-the-art technology (often dangerous anyway) or always taking the latest management theories from your newly qualified MBA graduates. It is about making the space in the culture of the law firm to develop a strategic plan, to update the plan in the light of experience and (crucially) to make sure that the plan can be implemented.

The legal services markets are changing faster now than at any time and the pace of change is likely to accelerate. Clients, we know, are increasingly demanding and we also know that this is not necessarily for the good, but they are rightly demanding a more commercial focus in legal services. The profession has some way to go to meet that demand.

If the legal markets significantly deregulate, and they might do so, then some law firms will simply be washed away in the flood tide. The new legal services providers that enter these markets with new channels of delivery, new technology and new work practices will demonstrate to their clients what having a commercial focus is really about.

There is no reason to dwell on the reasons (or excuses) for the position that law firms find themselves in today. It is possible to argue against my point of view. It is also not the case that every client is clamouring for a different type of service. There is a real concern that law firms will be left behind. It is time for more positive signs of change and innovation.

Talking to lawyers in law firms they say, for example, that their P.I. policy is a significant brake on their ability to be innovative or more commercial. This is at least partly true. But to what extent have these law firms ever asked their clients whether they would welcome a more risk-based approach to giving advice?

Many clients would actually appreciate being asked this question and, in return, if their lawyers were willing to take on more risk, it should also be possible to reach a sensible accommodation that would protect the P.I. position.

Incidentally the concept of the awkward customer is interesting. Many lawyers joke that they would be much better able to do their jobs without any clients at all! I hope this does not subconsciously deter innovation and change. I know that some clients are a nightmare, but you do not deal with a nightmare client by ignoring the problems they create and you

147

certainly should not justify failing to adapt to changing demands by blaming a minority of difficult people.

Many times I have spoken with senior partners and asked why their client's perception is that they needed to be more commercially minded.

Their riposte is usually that we, in-house lawyers and our businesses, would sue them when they got it wrong.

I wonder though whether this really is the case. In all the years I have worked as an in-house lawyer and through all the meetings I have ever had with other in-house lawyers, I cannot recall one instance when we discussed suing a law firm. There are disputes of course and some significant failings, but businesses do not tend to sue their legal advisers.

This issue of protecting the P.I. insurer has become an excuse not to challenge the status quo rather than a shield to protect against a legitimate threat.

All of these factors, whatever the reasons for them, amount to a general attitude that appears to say, 'Change is all too difficult'.

Maybe it is legal training that makes us so wary of change, but then again we are generally so good at being innovative and creative for our clients.

After a great deal of thought the conclusion is that, given all the talent at the profession's disposal, the law firms either do not want to change or are not interested enough in the benefits of changing.

Many law firms will only make significant progress to modernise when some of them go to the wall!

It is to be hoped that is not the case, but for those firms who are now positively on the road to adapting, changing and developing new and different services for their clients, good luck and just pedal a little faster.

The management issue

This book is not about the social or gender demographics of law firms. There are people far more qualified than me to comment on such issues. My perception of law firms in such matters is a relevant factor in the overall image a firm portrays.

It would be trite to simply criticise law firms for failing to promote and encourage their staff who are not male, middle aged and middle class. What is interesting is whether law firms take any account of the signals given to their clients about the results of their employment policies and practices.

On the positive side there are now as many women entering the profession as men (in fact slightly more women than men are qualifying at the moment). The profession is right to set the highest standards in the demands it places on entrants both as to their expertise and their commitment to clients.

The struggle is in understanding why general management is still such a low priority for many lawyers and law firms and that senior management positions are often given to people without managerial experience.

It is also still very much the case that the working of long and unsociable hours is praiseworthy, while leaving the office early to collect the kids from school is, at best, tolerated.

I know that it will always be the case that occasional late nights are inevitable, but they should not be the norm.

The result brought about over many years is a culture that encourages people to spoil their family life in favour of corporate activity on behalf of clients, many of whom (if they had the choice) would not want their lawyers, and certainly not their own staff, working through the night.

Given the huge investment law firms make in training and developing the legal skills of their staff, it seems bizarre that law firms persist in policies that almost certainly discourage significant numbers of their employees from building long term and mutually rewarding careers.

If law firms can remain profitable given these circumstances, it is possible that there is not enough incentive to change. If client perception matters, then law firms should know that clients believe many current work practices to be inefficient, costly and destructive.

Conclusions

Five issues. None are rocket science and will not be a surprise to anyone. The competitive forces at work in the profession today are significant and have resulted in many changes, most for the better. What is also true, however, is that much of the competition is only between law firms. Being better than the competition is not an indication of being anything like as effective and efficient as may be needed in the not too distant future.

There is perhaps a period of no more than five years for law firms to demonstrate that they are able to compete not just with their fellow law firms, but also with the new providers of legal services that will surely emerge.

Chapter Eleven

Opportunities for improving value, the in-house teams

The previous chapter began with a warning about a rant. In the interests of balance in-house lawyers should not escape criticism at this critical time either!

I am full of respect and admiration for this most dynamic and interesting sector of the profession. The role and the benefits good in-house legal services bring to businesses and to the wider profession has already been explained.

There are weaknesses, however, and these must be addressed.

A chain is only as strong as its weakest link and the profession, ultimately, is only as strong as the weakest constituent part. In-house lawyers have come a long way in the last twenty years, but the journey should not end with the reputation and influence so far achieved. Improvements should still be made and I believe there are three specific criticisms that should be addressed:

- Too many senior in-house lawyers are poor managers and do not properly develop either themselves or their staff,

- Too many in-house lawyers make thoughtless demands of their external colleagues in law firms, and

- Too few in-house lawyers have made it to the boardroom.

Poor managers

Management is not just about fighting fires or about being able to spend lots of money on expensive external advice. Yet sometimes in conversation with some senior in-house lawyers you would think that these were the most important in defining their value.

Management should be about developing the awareness in the business not to repeat mistakes and managing the risk that businesses have to take to be competitive. Management is also about encouraging and facilitating staff to fulfil their potential, and being able to recognise and reward talent throughout a team.

Over the years I have picked up some 'do's' and some 'don'ts' from many conversations with in-house lawyers and those that work with them.

First, some fairly typical 'don'ts' for the senior in-house lawyers who do not inspire:

- Don't cut yourself off from your team in a remote corner office

- Don't spend the day planning how to get more recognition for yourself and neglecting what is happening outside your door

- Don't stifle ingenuity and innovation by overbearing process or bureaucracy

- Don't allow the ineffectual or the incompetent to lower standards or morale

- Don't neglect the business areas just because you have less contact with them than before

- Don't ever let your team believe you care less

- Don't get stale and stay in post

- Don't disguise shortcomings in the team by outsourcing

Second, some fairly typical 'do's' for the senior in-house lawyers who do inspire:

- Do always delegate to the lowest level of competence

- Do stand behind your team when they need your support

- Do let them go forward when they don't need your support

- Do design the strategic profile of the work that you do

- Do develop and encourage your staff

- Do be visible, thoughtful and proactive

- Do build the resilience in expertise and experience within the team so that the business can be supported whatever the circumstances may be

- Do find the time to respect and appreciate the contribution people make

- Do set the highest standards and show that standards will be maintained

- Do outsource when it is right to do so, at the right time and to the right firms.

These two lists are self-explanatory, but there is a theme that runs through both of them. It is that above all, the really good lawyers never let the stature of the businesses they work in become an excuse for arrogance or unreasonableness in their dealings with others.

Trust and credibility always comes from the way lawyers work and not those they work for. This leads us on to my second criticism.

Unreasonable demands

This is the one thing about some in-house lawyers that really disappoints. It disappoints because in a sense it hints at the fact that perhaps some in-house lawyers do not recognise the struggle this sector of the profession has had in years gone by. It suggests that some may not have learnt the lessons that they, above all, really should have fully understood. It is about arrogance.

For years the profession treated in-house lawyers in a shoddy way. We were not paranoid. They really didn't like us!

We have seen this attitude change. If anything, in-house lawyers now are the ones in the pre-eminent position. Not because they are better lawyers, but because they have become the holders of the corporate purse strings and therefore possess the spending power.

In these circumstances it is possible to see why arrogance has become a factor. Arrogance, however, is just so terribly destructive of value.

I have no difficulty putting law firms through the most exacting selection procedures, no problem with wanting to be shown where value lies and no doubt that law firms have a long road to travel to be fully aware of their clients' needs. I do not believe that it is arrogant to hold such views.

What is difficult to accept is, for example, inviting busy partners in law firms to travel long distances to head-offices to meet the senior lawyer, who is then suddenly too busy for the meeting and a poorly briefed subordinate steps in instead;

• or demanding, for example, access to a law firm's library facilities when access is already available elsewhere and it is not needed;

• or wanting bespoke seminars developed and presented for their teams, but then having only half the attendance they predicted;

• or wrapping up incompetence or laziness in the cloak of urgent instructions to placate a frustrated business team.

These all happen and law firms are full of stories where their disappointment borders on contempt. It is not the norm and surely it is not the conduct that thousands of in-house lawyers have ever demonstrated, but the concern is simple. Reputations are hard won and easily lost.

What made the in-house sector so respected (cost effective, relevant and timely advice that meets genuine need) will keep the in-house sector respected. Do not let that hard won reputation be lost.

The relationship with law firms is a vital one. It is vital for the businesses concerned, for the instructing team and for the law firm. As we have seen before, developing the right strategy begins with understanding the interests of all involved. 'Mutual gains' is the phrase adopted by Professor Fisher and is certainly my preferred approach. In-house lawyers who neglect the interests of the law firm or subjugate those interests entirely to the interests of the in-house lawyers/businesses do themselves, their businesses and the profession a significant disservice.

Arrogance is ignorant of interests and therefore destructive of creativity and value for all concerned.

The boardroom?

The boardroom is the preferred, but sadly elusive, destination of many senior in-house lawyers. The question such lawyers must answer is why with every boardroom having at least one accountant (and sometimes several) so few lawyers make it to the top table.

The answer I think lies in three weaknesses;

•   Being a clever lawyer does not translate automatically into being good in business.

•   Lawyers value themselves in ways that are less valued by business people.

•   Lawyers are just not very good at presenting their efforts so that they can be valued by business people.

We have seen all three weaknesses before in the analysis of the *perception test.*

Even though in-house lawyers tend to be more in tune with the needs of the businesses they work in than their counterparts in law firms there is still, evidently, a significant perception gap between lawyers in-house and their non-lawyer colleagues.

155

Take the following three statements. None are either fair or accurate, but they reflect the sentiments of many business people and result in a perception deficit that the lawyers must make up. At best lawyers have failed to address these issues and at worst they have actually encouraged them to persist.

- Accountants talk the language of risk; lawyers talk the language of potential liability.

- Accountants can be creative saving money; lawyers find problems that cost money.

- Accountants are an essential requirement of good fiscal and corporate governance; lawyers are not essential for any positive reason and only become useful when things have already gone wrong.

If you were the chief executive of a busy, dynamic and ambitious company, and surrounded by people who held these sorts of views, would you want a lawyer at your board table? I suspect not.

Lawyers can and should play a key strategic role in businesses. Their contribution is at least as skilful, valuable and important as any contribution made by any accountant. The problem is that lawyers do not (maybe will not) talk the language of business people.

Until lawyers begin to fulfil their potential by visibly and proactively managing strategic risk for their businesses and ally that skill with an appreciation of what is a valuable contribution in the perception of those businesses, they are destined to remain on the fringes of the corporate world.

Hopefully this situation will change. It is possible that this is the next phase in the evolution of the in-house lawyer and it is just a matter of time before lawyers break through.

Encouragingly it appears to be the case that CEOs in North America do value the contribution made by their in-house general counsel. However, at present we are not even on the radar screen of the playmakers that matter and I suspect that the situation will not change dramatically until we all start to see the world through their eyes.

Conclusions

The best in-house lawyers, like the best lawyers in law firms, are brilliant. They provide an invaluable service and deserve all they receive.

It would be foolish to pretend, however, that in-house lawyers have reached a stage where acclaim can be uncritical. There are gaps in their skills and those gaps become more obvious when senior in-house lawyers are compared directly with their accountancy colleagues.

This is most obvious in the failure of lawyers to break through into the boardroom. For as long as lawyers complain that their businesses do not understand their contribution, the situation will not improve. It is not business that is at fault, but the lawyers who cannot adapt their message so that their worth becomes visible and valuable.

Chapter Twelve

Top ten tips

Some people may consider the last two chapters unduly critical of certain aspects of the service provided by lawyers today. Hopefully they will see the comments to be destructively critical or driven by a wish to 'do down' the contribution of the legal profession.

To redress the balance somewhat the next two chapters explore the best ways to maximise the talent and the very positive contribution that can be made by in-house lawyers and lawyers in firms working together for the benefit of themselves and, above all, for the benefit of their clients.

This chapter looks at the factors that make up the essential characteristics of outstanding lawyers and outstanding legal services. The next chapter looks at the best way to organise legal services to make the best use of the skills and talents available.

First though, my personal top ten tips for outstanding legal services:

1. Have a strategy for how best to deliver the service.

2. Have a communication strategy.

3. Develop all staff to maximise their potential.

4. Define the client's meaning of value and avoid imposing the house style.

5. Invest time in innovation but not at the expense of relationships and emotional intelligence.

6. Understand the client's perception of your actions and modify behaviour accordingly.

7. Train soft skills.

8. Assume nothing. Build team resilience to answer the 'what ifs'.

9. Always, always keep commitments.

10. Smile!

While compiling this list and considering all the various and numerous components of an outstanding legal service, one thing became apparent beyond the obvious one of just how hard it is to define excellence. (We all know when something is brilliant, but describing why it is so is never as easy as recognising brilliance in the first place.) The issue that stood out (or rather did not stand out) was just how little consideration I gave to the actual quality of the legal expertise on offer in deciding what made for an outstanding service.

I am not being obtuse in not regarding the quality of legal expertise to be a top ten issue.

This may be because I am used to buying legal services from law firms where the level of expertise is nearly always assured. In a sense, therefore, some views might be misleading, as no doubt there are many purchasers of legal services who do have to consider whether the right level of legal expertise is available from a particular law firm.

Even when this is the case, identifying the lawyers with the required level of legal expertise is simply the qualifying hurdle for law firms to become eligible for more detailed consideration and selection.

The key selection criteria that determine who wins and who loses therefore discounts legal expertise in nearly all cases.

The issues uppermost in the minds of those making the selection are such things as rapport, empathy, commerciality and communication. It is the lawyer's performance against these indicators that determines excellence.

All this reconfirms one of the early points made in this book about the client's perception of what really matters in a relationship with a lawyer.

Legal expertise is not the clinching factor by any means and this explains why legal expertise is not in my top ten tips.

So what are the clinching factors that make for an outstanding legal service?

160

1. Delivery

My number one top tip is to define the strategy for service delivery.

It does not matter what area of law is involved or what type of transaction is being considered; delivery is the key to success.

'Delivery' in this sense means appreciating who is to receive the advice, when they are to receive it and how it should be given. These three elements should be understood in advance, strategies developed to meet the expectations of the client and resources given to ensure that those expectations are met.

If these three elements of service delivery are addressed satisfactorily, the relationship between client and lawyer will be valued and valuable to all concerned.

All lawyers should always have at the front of their minds that the delivery of their service is the very best time to impress a client and one of the few times when the client is able to make a rational value judgement of the quality of lawyer and the service given.

A personal mantra to sum up the essence of excellence in legal services is 'Delivery, Delivery, Delivery'!

2. Communication

Everyone knows this is important and yet when relationships break down it is the lack of proper and effective communication that is nearly always cited as a contributory factor.

Communication should be elevated to the level where there is a conscious element of planning to ensure that it is always thoughtful and relevant.

The issues that must be addressed are:

- Who should be communicating with whom to ensure that instructions are clear and information is accessible?

- When should people communicate and how should they communicate to avoid unnecessary costs but maximise the value of the work that has been done?

- What are the client's preferences?

- How can those preferences be incorporated into the communication strategy without compromising the adequacy of the service and the skill and care required?

Communication *within* the legal department and the law firm is also really important, particularly where the relationship with the client operates at different levels. All lawyers should be aware of all the work being done on behalf of a client and communications should then be targeted so that the client is not bombarded with too many messages or, worse, inconsistent messages.

Finally it should be the aim of all lawyers to develop and revisit their communication strategy in the light of experience. It is, after all, an opportunity to demonstrate to the client that there is thought and care involved on the part of the lawyer and it is probably the most tangible way a client can appreciate and value the service that they are given.

3. Develop staff

The business of the law is all about personal relationships (this probably will change, and probably should change, but for now the perceived strength of the personal relationship between lawyer and client is probably the biggest factor in determining whether the client believes the service to be good, bad or just indifferent).

It is therefore perhaps not surprising that the really good relationships are jealously guarded by the lawyers who own them. They seem to believe that their particular kind of client only wants to deal with them.

To an extent this is true and familiarity is certainly a big factor for many clients. It is also true that many relationships fray at the edges as soon as a new lawyer is introduced.

What then tends to happen is a self-fulfilling 'Catch 22' where the client only likes dealing with a particular lawyer because every other lawyer is so unfamiliar and the lawyer does not want other lawyers involved because the client does not want to deal with anyone else.

In truth, while this is a very familiar picture, it represents a very weak business model.

The lawyer with the good relationship often finds that he or she is tied to doing work that should be delegated. The firm is vulnerable to the client leaving the business when the lawyer moves on. Staff who should have an exposure to real people are held back for too long while the partner takes care of the client relationship issues. It also means that the client is left to feel exposed if the lawyer is absent for any length of time (even to the extent of the lawyer having to leave contact details when he or she is on holiday or ill). Finally if things go wrong between lawyer and client, the problem can be too easily hidden and can be left to drift for too long before action is taken.

I apply the following rule of thumb to teams. If there is good news to give the client, then the most junior member of the team involved in the transaction should give the client the good news. If there is bad news to give or if a problem is encountered, then the most senior member of the team should inform the client.

It is important for the client to see and have contact with the right number of people. It means there is an opportunity to build resource and expertise resilience into the approach the firm adopts. It also means that lawyers at all levels of experience begin to see and value the importance of the client relationship and the factors that make each client relationship work well. It engenders a proper sense of team worth and values all contributions. It also allows the lawyers to manage the work down to the most appropriate level of experience without unsettling the client. For all these reasons it is a sure sign of a mature and effective legal service when all the staff involved with a client have a visible contribution to make.

4. Defining value

If you have not taken the time and trouble to define what the client will value by virtue of your involvement with his or her business, then you trust to luck and intuition.

The absence of either or both of these fickle elements in a relationship (and neither is obviously guaranteed!) will result in a potentially dysfunctional service. The extent to which it is bad or just indifferent will be seen in how long the relationship ultimately lasts and the extent to which billing is discounted to placate anger, distrust or incredulity.

Any failure to take the trouble to define the client's perception of value is therefore directly and sometimes permanently destructive of value.

I do not like the house-style approach of some law firms where they seem to believe that their particular brand of legal service is so good that 'one size fits all'. In these firms the client's preferences relating to communication, billing and service delivery are relegated behind the preferred approach of the lawyers.

The house style should only be adopted when it is what the client wants.

5. Invest time in innovation but not at the expense of emotional intelligence

Every type of business can improve its efficiency and effectiveness by the skilful and thoughtful use of technology.

It is common sense to suggest that clients want to see technology deployed by law firms to save money and improve effectiveness. Clients, however, do not want to see technology placed between themselves and their legal team as some kind of computer-generated barricade where emotional intelligence is sacrificed for the overbearing use of the latest gizmo.

Technology does not have all the answers (and never will have all the answers). The best lawyers instinctively know how to apply their expertise to best effect. There is a sense in which they *feel* the solution that is right for their client.

164

In many ways this is one of the great strengths of our profession. It is the value added magic ingredient that comes from the thoughtful mix of knowledge, expertise, communication and delivery.

Technology has a vital role to fulfil at the heart of the profession. It will save costs, prevent waste and avoid inaccuracy, but it should never replace the emotional intelligence that allows lawyers to make value judgements.

I do not want to get misty eyed but it is the lawyers' sense of equity and justice, not a computer programme, that must be preserved at all costs and trumpeted wherever possible.

Invest in technology to commodotise processes, to cut out waste and to develop systems based solutions for the routine and the transactional. But do not sacrifice the passion to pursue solutions, the passion to represent or the passion to care.

Let us recognise and be proud of the fact that lawyers have unique qualities that should never be replaced by hardware or software solutions.

The clever bit is to get the balance right; we must not reject technology solutions because of arrogance about these unique qualities nor should we embrace all the new fangled technologies in the rush for efficiency at the expense of those unique qualities.

6. Understand the client's perception and adapt behaviour accordingly

The secret of all successful businesses anywhere, in any industry, at any time?

Give the punters what they want.

It's a bit like Basil Fawlty exclaiming that his wife's specialist subject on Mastermind would be "Statements of the bleeding obvious"! But obvious or not, lawyers do not pay enough attention to what their clients' want and consistently give the service that they, the lawyers, want to give.

There are echoes of tip number 4 'Defining value', but this point goes wider.

When a client reacts badly to a letter or a call or a particular development, it is very unlikely that they are doing so out of malevolence or deliberate awkwardness. The likelihood is, in fact, that the lawyer did not appreciate an entirely predictable reaction because he or she failed to perceive the situation from the client's perspective.

If only lawyers put themselves in the client's position, they would act differently more often. Probably saying the same but in a different way.

I know of law firms that routinely discount perfectly valid bills because of client dissatisfaction with wholly avoidable issues. Buying client satisfaction, however, is very expensive. It is also entirely unnecessary especially when it is the case that most clients give this away for free to those lawyers who can see the world through their eyes.

7. Have a strategy to train soft skills

Which of these two statements do you think will impress a client the most?

"He's a really good lawyer. No one knows their subject better"

Or

"He's a really good lawyer. He really knows what the client wants and gives it to them every time"

It is obvious isn't it? And yet at all levels in every law firm and in-house departments too, there will be pockets of resistance to anything that strays from teaching black letter law and into the preaching of airy fairy psycho-babble (as it is invariably characterised).

Knowing black letter law, however, does not equip anyone to know how to present, how to listen, how to help the client see the issues, how to help the client define his or her requirements, how to evaluate risk.

It is these skills that are so often lacking but it is these same skills that are needed by all lawyers if their service is to be considered outstanding.

These are the skills, therefore, that must be systematically and routinely trained at all levels in the profession from graduate trainee through to managing partner.

These are the skills that are the currency of profitability and excellence.

8. Assume nothing!

Being good is about getting things right.

Getting things right, however, for the majority of law firms and in-house teams is a relatively routine event.

In the ordinary course of events resources are matched to meet the demand, the transaction proceeds, the transaction completes, the client accepts the bill and the client pays the bill. This is good, but being outstanding is about getting things right when the relatively routine is not the norm, for example, when the client is ambushed by a hostile bid, when the lead partner defects to another firm, when the computers crash at a critical point. Cliché or not, every crisis is an opportunity to shine and the outstanding shine brightest of all.

Being outstanding is about shining in a crisis and the firms that have assumed nothing and asked the "what ifs" know what to do in a crisis. They respond, reassure and still deliver.

If you are able to handle a crisis well, to rise to the occasion and to show that the client's crisis is shared, then the client's loyalty is virtually assured.

Yet too many law firms and even in-house teams do not respond well in a crisis. They do not have a contingency for the partner who defects or the in-house lawyer who goes off sick, because they have not developed the team's profile or had a communication strategy that reassured. They do not have partners wired to work from home if the need is there...

They have not understood that the client is not only buying a service; they are also buying an insurance policy that says, 'We will handle it' whatever happens.

Everyone should be good, but only a few will be outstanding.

167

Prepare to be outstanding and your preparation will not be in vain.

9. Always, always keep commitments

Life is about making commitments, being a lawyer is about keeping them.

Trust is like the air in our lungs. You cannot see it or touch it, but let it go and the body will die.

Clients expect more from lawyers than they do from many other service providers and long may that be so. It is, however, essential that the commitments a lawyer makes are kept if the trust that is essential between lawyer and client is to be maintained and enhanced.

"I will call you back later today"

"The report will be on your desk at 4pm"

"I will make the meeting"

"Completion is Friday"

Every commitment made is an I.O.U. of service promised. Every commitment kept is then the currency of trust that repays the I.O.U. Every commitment missed is a bounced cheque of expectations dashed and disappointment.

Very often clients are vulnerable in front of their lawyers. It is uncomfortable to feel vulnerable. Commitments made and kept help clients deal with their insecurities and it should never be underestimated just how important it is to ensure that clients are not let down in any way by their lawyers.

10. Smile!

Obvious isn't it?

It is a slightly frivolous point to make, but one that experience says is always underestimated.

It is always better to deal with cheerful people. It is always easier to cope with difficult problems if there is some humour to keep everyone going. It is, frankly, harder to sack a lawyer who is personable than one who is arrogant and aloof.

These are my top ten tips to delivering an outstanding legal service. They are a personal selection, though influenced by the best law firms I have worked with and the best in-house lawyers I have managed or I have been managed by.

The law is full of incredible people; people with whom I am proud to be associated even if only by virtue of a shared profession. Why they are incredible is because more often than not they measure up to standards of work and relationship management that is simply outstanding by any standards.

The next chapter sets out the best model for service delivery.

Chapter Thirteen

A new model army?

This book represents something of a journey through various aspects of relationship management explaining the opportunities and the pitfalls for lawyers, whose clients will always want them to aspire to provide an outstanding legal service.

The question not yet answered is what does it all mean in the real world, away from management theory, best practice and expert consultants?

What does the requirement for realising value mean for the way we are organised, the way we work and the way we relate to our colleagues, our rivals and our clients?

This chapter sets out a model for the delivery of legal services that seeks to maximise the contribution of both in-house lawyers and lawyers in law firms.

The in-house offering

As we have seen, in-house lawyers offer much to their employing businesses. The in-house legal team, however, is very unlikely (with limited resources and expertise in all areas) to be able to offer a comprehensive legal service in its own right.

It is important to identify the significant strengths on which to build the profile and the reputation of the in-house legal team. The following list represents some of the clear and key advantages over lawyers in law firms:

- Privileged access to all business areas and all personnel

- In-depth client knowledge

- In-depth appreciation of core risk areas

- Expert selection of law firms and expert managers of outsourced legal work

It seems obvious that these are unique qualities that only the in-house lawyer can hope to develop to a strategically significant degree. It is these qualities that should shape the type of legal service the in-house lawyer provides.

The law firm offering

Like in-house lawyers, law firms have so much to offer their corporate clients. Their strengths, however, are different to those of in-house lawyers and the key to their success is to find ways in which to unlock the value they offer. The key advantages law firms have over in-house lawyers are:

- A much broader range of experience and expertise across many disciplines

- Capacity and resources that can be mobilised to meet fluctuations in demand

- Economies of scale across process, expertise and technology

These are powerful credentials to support the need to manage risk in business and to provide legal services solutions when required. There are depths of resource and levels of expertise available in law firms that simply cannot be consistently matched by any in-house legal team.

Stronger than the sum of their parts

Major corporate clients require a range of legal services, some predictable some not, some routine some strategic, some carrying significant risk some not, some costly some not. This range of work will require different strengths and different skills. It is very likely therefore that for most corporate clients, at different times, the relative merits of law firms and in-house lawyers will need to be considered.

The facility to select the right lawyer for the right job by using resources in-house or externally (or a combination of the two) is a phenomenon only of relatively recent times. It has opened up new areas of work as well as new ways of working (all to the advantage of clients generally). What is needed therefore is not only an appreciation of the strengths of different lawyers but the characteristics of different types of legal work.

There are four significant categories of work:

- **Bulk.** This is usually characterised as non-strategic, high volume, relatively low risk, low cost and highly cost sensitive. There is only a small requirement for in-depth client knowledge. The work is also process and systems driven with a significant use of technology.

Examples of work in this category would be debt collection, mortgage related litigation and mortgage related conveyancing.

- **Transactional.** This is usually characterised as non-strategic, medium risk work that is regular but not necessarily routine in nature. It is process and systems adapted to maximise efficiency. In-depth client knowledge is usually required and the work is very cost sensitive.

Examples of work in this category would be most types of commercial work, but particularly contract negotiation.

- **Non-core specialist.** This work is usually strategically significant and high risk. It may be slightly esoteric or at least unusual. Some client knowledge is certainly required. It is unlikely that this work will be cost sensitive.

An example of work in this category would be high profile litigation.

- **Core specialist.** This is also strategically significant and high risk (often reputational risk is a key factor in this type of work). It is work that is regularly required and in depth knowledge of the client is essential. The work does not tend to be cost sensitive.

Examples of work in this category would be client specific regulatory and compliance work, client specific product development and corporate governance issues.

In graphical terms, *fig 11* shows how these categories relate to each other in the context of work that is either more suitable for law firms or more suitable for in-house lawyers.

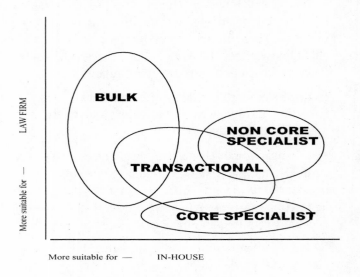

Looking at this more closely:

Bulk work

It can never be an effective use of an in-house team to undertake bulk work of any nature. None of the key advantages of an in-house lawyer are utilised and the key advantages of the law firm are a much better match for the profile of this type of work.

There are a number of lending institutions, for example, that began to develop expertise in bulk processing of legal work in the late eighties and into the nineties. Their general expertise in human resource management and systems or process design allowed them to build effective debt recovery or remortgage machines. These operations, however, were always subject to the vagaries of demand with many staff being periodically overwhelmed with work or with little to do.

Nearly all these lenders now outsource this type of work to law firms that have developed considerable expertise in this area. The risk of variable demand has been passed to the law firms who can to some extent mitigate the risk by managing work on behalf of many different clients.

There is also more incentive for law firms to invest in updating systems given the volumes of work available and the economies that come from scale. Provided costs are managed down to an acceptable (low) level it is clearly much better for the lenders to outsource this work.

Non-core specialist work

Similarly non-core specialist work is a much better match for the law firm's key advantages.

To employ an expensive in-house lawyer with specialist skills that are rarely used runs an unattractive risk in terms of maintaining that expertise but is unlikely, in any case, ever to make economic sense.

Even if the in-house lawyer were able to do some of the work involved, the limited nature of support and back up in-house would make it impractical.

Transactional work

This is more difficult to be categorical about and there are many in-house lawyers who make a very valuable contribution to their employer businesses by negotiating, for example, commercial contracts for I.T. acquisition.

It is the case, however, that the profile of this work is better suited to law firms. The missing ingredient, and why in-house lawyers still play a significant role with this type of work, is cost.

Law firms clearly have more resources and are likely to have more in-depth expertise, but they are also very expensive, particularly for work that might not be high risk or strategically significant. It is this cost factor that is at present the issue for most businesses when deciding whether work is outsourced or undertaken in-house.

The problem with most law firms is that they still tackle routine corporate commercial work on a traditional charging structure predominantly using hourly rates. As we have seen before, hourly rates are perceived by clients as creating inefficiencies and stifling innovation.

If (hopefully *when*) law firms can invent the charging mechanisms that overcome these impediments, I believe there are seriously significant amounts of work that can, should and probably will be outsourced to them.

Core specialist work

While this is undeniably work that law firms can perform to an acceptable standard, it is also work that exactly matches the key advantages of in-house lawyers.

The model reflects the fact that both sectors of the profession are suitable homes for core specialist work but it will always be the case that business clients prefer their own in-house lawyers to be responsible for this work rather than external suppliers of legal services.

It is advisable for any in-house lawyer to concentrate on developing expertise in core specialist areas and to develop the strategies that demonstrate the considerable value he or she adds by virtue of this expertise.

What does this mean?

There are clear categories of work that are more or less suited to law firms on the one hand and in-house legal teams on the other hand.

We can also see that, where work should be outsourced, two things happen:

- First: the in-house team becomes an essential entry

point into the client for the law firm to be able to relate to the client and develop a profile with the client.

• Second: the in-house team's role changes from being the supplier of legal services to being the expert manager of legal services.

In short, whether work is done in-house or by the law firm, there is a mutually supporting, almost symbiotic, relationship that should maximise the key advantages of both in-house lawyers and law firms. This in turn results in comprehensive service coverage for clients with an opportunity to manage both risk and cost across the broad range of legal and regulatory issues affecting businesses.

On this basis, it is possible to profile the shape and responsibilities of the ideal in-house legal team. Its essential characteristics are likely to be:

• Relatively small in number. Big enough to cover the core specialisms but small enough to be non-bureaucratic and nimble.

• Having key specialist skills to support core business activities with resilience within teams to be able to support each other in times of significant workload pressure.

• Proactive risk managers freed from routine legal work and actively educating and supporting their business colleagues to manage risk as effectively as possible.

• Lawyers with project manager skills to be able to apply risk management and creative skills in the context of multi-disciplinary projects undertaken by their businesses.

• Outsourcers of bulk work to law firms that in turn can manage their overheads to reduce the cost per case to the lowest sustainable level practicable.

• Outsourcers of non-core specialist work to law firms where there is proven expertise

- Outsourcers of transactional work provided there is sufficient innovation around the issue of costs that in turn will free the in-house lawyers to assume the proactive role that best suits their key skills.

- Fully integrated into the culture of their businesses.

This profile of an in-house legal team is crammed full of opportunity for all lawyers and it is full of potential value for their clients.

The law is one of only a few dynamics in business that can be said to have true strategic significance. Its active management to identify and deal with risk while being cost effective and always sensitive to the needs of the businesses involved is the great challenge for all lawyers.

In-house lawyers do not have all the answers nor do law firms. By maximising their different skills and contributions, lawyers in-house and in law firms can together become a most respected and essential ally of corporate clients everywhere.

Chapter Fourteen

The biggest challenges are yet to come

The beginning of the last chapter described this book as something of a personal journey. It is also a journey describing the progress of lawyers as creative problem solvers through the last twenty to thirty years. For the legal profession it is a journey which has yet to end and where even the destination is far from certain.

It must be quite difficult for senior partners in our biggest law firms. Many of them have been incredibly successful in recent times, perhaps beyond their dreams, but what next? Planning for change after a period of success is the hardest thing to do, but planning for change is a necessity if success is to continue.

As they look out from their top floor offices across the City of London or the major city centres of the UK, what future do they see? In the last ten years there has been massive growth in demand for legal services, great increases in income and a new energy in the economy to develop and grow. But what of the next five years, what next do they think will happen?

I certainly do not know what will happen.

As the old saying goes, there are only two great certainties, 'death' and 'taxes'. To this can be added a third, 'change'.

Change is constant and change will always be a factor. To what extent it is a factor for good or ill is as much a question of attitude as it is a question of circumstance.

While it is not clear what will happen over the next five years, it is likely that in even this short period of time we will potentially see the most far reaching and fundamental changes to the legal profession there have ever been.

If I am right, then the senior partners of today may have less time than they think for looking out of their office windows!

Spinning faster and faster

There is a well known Chinese proverb to reflect upon;

The old emperor has a problem that all the academics and all the wise men of the time have failed to solve. A great reward of gold and silks is offered to anyone who can solve the problem.

A poor man offers to help. He says he knows the answer.

The legend says that the poor man does indeed know the answer and he tells the emperor what the emperor has waited a lifetime to hear.

The emperor offers the poor man great riches, but the poor man wants a different prize. He wants the emperor to give him a chessboard and on the first square of the chessboard he asks the emperor to place a single grain of rice.

On the second square he wants the emperor to place just two grains of rice. On the third square there must be four gains of rice, on the next square eight grains and so on. On each subsequent square the number of rice grains is to be doubled, until the sixty-fourth square is reached.

The emperor is astonished at the lack of ambition in the poor man to want so little, but in return for the right answer to his most intractable problem, he readily agrees to give the poor man his silly little prize.

Less than half way through the sixty-four squares all the rice in China has been given away.

The story points to how complacent we can all become even in the face of circumstances that are evident for all to see. It is also a salutary warning that to ignore what is obvious may potentially overwhelm us.

All the new technologies that are available to us today are like the grains of rice on the chessboard.

There are technologies that have transformed the way we live. We see this obviously in the way the world communicates and in the way the world does business. It is much harder to say that these new technologies have so far transformed the way we work in the legal world.

The pace of change is getting faster and faster and we may have a sense of being overtaken by our own shortcomings when it comes to trying to understand what is happening. It does not bode well.

My concern for the business of the law is that in no sense has the profession ever really embraced change as a positive and decisive factor in developing new work, new markets and new ways to deliver existing services.

Lawyers treat change with great suspicion. We all know people who still get their secretaries to print off their emails so that they can have a pile of paper on their desks. To the extent that new technologies are deployed in the way we work, it has been a grudging and slow process.

This is really quite depressing. It is right to exercise caution against adopting every single new fangled gimmick that was ever invented, but lawyers are so far off the pace when it comes to innovative technology solutions that it is only the fact that the whole profession is so backward that disguises the ineptitude.

I really am very nervous for the profession. The business of the law is so important. It is part of the foundation of a just and civilised society. It represents and protects the freedoms of the individual. It ensures that the wheels of commerce can turn with certainty. It is also, despite all the criticisms, one of the few areas of working life where the public still expect the highest standards of ethical behaviour and where very largely those expectations are met.

And yet despite this essential and pivotal role in the business and social consciousness of our lives, lawyers lack the business skills and the entrepreneurial guile to maximise the benefits provided by the new technologies and the new ways of working and therefore the new opportunities to deliver value.

So what?

Well, for the last twenty years, 'so what?' would be a justified response. The profession has been, and still is, protected by regulation. The ivory towers occupied by so many have also been impressive fortresses against invaders. The attitude has almost been 'If we all stick together lads, we can carry on as we have always done'. There are still, after all, respected senior lawyers who believe that the domestic conveyancing market would be so much better if the monopolistic price fixing cartels of the seventies could be restored! And they say so without a hint of irony.

But, but, but...

In the next five years there is every chance that the ivory towers will crumble as protective (anti-competitive) regulations are removed.

In particular the rule that in-house lawyers may not (except in very narrow circumstances) act for the clients of their employer businesses is one that will come under the closest scrutiny.

At first glance this rather innocuous looking rule might be easily overlooked. So what if the odd lawyer does a bit of work for someone other than his or her employer? Besides, there are not too many in-house lawyers today who would actually want to act for their employer's customers.

But think on this;

- Does it not mean that new corporations could be formed specifically to deliver legal services?

- Does it not mean that law firms will be in competition not just with other law firms but also with commercial undertakings of every size, shape and type?

- Does it not mean that all the competitive forces of the twenty-first century will be unleashed on a profession that has barely come to terms with the twentieth century?

If you were the Chief Executive of a supermarket chain, or a roadside recovery service, or a global investment bank, or an international accountancy business, or a management consultancy, would you not stop to think if your customers would welcome a legal service as part of the package of products you might offer to them?

I would.

After all, it isn't fanciful to suppose that most people in a road accident would prefer to use the legal team of their insurer or their roadside recovery business.

Indeed most people might like to do their conveyancing through their local DIY superstore.

And if your company is doing a deal with another, why not use the Accountant's legal team or the Merchant Bank's lawyers?

Deregulation will come one day and when it does the law firms that charge by the hour, run litigation files at the convenience of their appointed QC and cannot remember how to spell the name of the client's managing director, will die.

"Courage, mon brave"

It is the combination of deregulation at the very time when new technologies and systems can now unlock the mysteries of legal process that presents such a significant challenge for the legal profession.

The banks used to circle the conveyancing market like oil wells that were once uneconomic to develop. Fifteen years ago they decided it was too expensive and too difficult to develop; today they might not see things the same way.

Lawyers who today have never had it so good may find that tomorrow they had just bit parts in an historical drama.

All this, of course might not be a bad thing.

There are two reasons for great optimism;

• There will clearly be many new opportunities for lawyers to work in different environments with different types of career.

- For those who want to offer legal services in the traditional ways there is still time to adapt and change.

Lawyers are an essential element in the social and economic mix that makes up what we call our society. This book is not about their role in civil or criminal justice, but in business. Here lawyers create, facilitate and conclude the biggest deals. They organise and protect their clients and ensure good governance. Their skills and dedication oil the machine that generates the wealth that makes our world what it is.

The world of business is not about to turn its back on these skills. They are essential.

What is not essential and what will inevitably change are the outdated procedures, processes and attitudes that in fact stifle innovation and creativity, but which for years have characterised elements of traditional legal services.

Law firms and in-house legal teams that embrace change and realise what their clients really value will survive and will flourish.

The new providers of legal services, whether they are supermarkets or accountancy firms or banks, will bring to the fore new ideas and new ways of working, but they too have lessons to learn. They will only survive if they can encapsulate the skills and the integrity of lawyers in the essence of technology and process driven solutions.

Everyone has much to learn from each other, but the true winners will be the lawyers, whose talents will at last have the opportunity to fulfil their very great potential, and, of course, the clients, who will receive legal services that are effective, efficient and full of value.

...And finally

Someone recently asked me if I had a vision for the legal profession.

If we start by accepting that one man's vision is another man's hallucination, here are a few thoughts to share.

Lawyers have made massive leaps forward in recent years. They have begun to understand that service is about more than knowing an answer. In this book I have tried to point out where mistakes are still made and where service can and must be improved.

I have described how in-house lawyers have in many ways shown the way forward for the whole profession and how they have developed different skills that all lawyers, wherever and however they practice, should emulate.

It is all about realising value; value for the lawyers and value for their clients. There is so much that has been done, but there is still so much more to do.

If now, law firms bask in the false after-glow of their current success, and if in-house legal teams fail to press home the needs of their clients that they are uniquely placed to understand, then lawyers will fail their clients as well as themselves.

If lawyers build on the progress they have made through recent years and realise the value their clients demand, the profession will thrive. It will thrive, however, not as it does today, but in many more varied, more stimulating and more effective ways, each approach finding the best way to deliver value to clients through the creative solutions of their lawyers.

Lawyers really do have a superior opportunity to do good and I am very confident that good will be done.

Printed in the United Kingdom
by Lightning Source UK Ltd.
1921